97 Things Every SRE Should Know

Collective Wisdom from the Experts

Emil Stolarsky and Jaime Woo

Beijing · Boston · Farnham · Sebastopol · Tokyo

97 Things Every SRE Should Know

by Emil Stolarsky and Jaime Woo

Published by O'Reilly Media, Inc., 1005 Gravenstein Highway North, Sebastopol, CA 95472.

O'Reilly books may be purchased for educational, business, or sales promotional use. Online editions are also available for most titles (*http://oreilly.com*). For more information, contact our corporate/institutional sales department: 800-998-9938 or *corporate@oreilly.com*.

Acquisitions Editor: John Devins	**Indexer:** nSight, Inc.
Developmental Editor: Corbin Collins	**Interior Designer:** David Futato
Production Editor: Beth Kelly	**Cover Designer:** Randy Comer
Copyeditor: nSight, Inc.	**Illustrator:** Kate Dullea
Proofreader: Shannon Turlington	

November 2020:   First Edition

Revision History for the First Edition
2020-11-18:   First Release

See *http://oreilly.com/catalog/errata.csp?isbn=9781492081494* for release details.

978-1-492-08149-4

[LSI]

Table of Contents

Part I.   New to SRE

Part II. Zero to One

Part III.   One to Ten

Part IV.   Ten to Hundred

Part V. The Future of SRE

Preface

If there is one defining trait of an SRE, it would be curiosity. There's something about trying to understand how a system works, bringing it back from failure, or generally improving it that tickles the parts of our brains where curiosity lives. This trait is probably common through most, if not all, engineering practices. There's a story we both love that seems to encompass this trait perfectly.

On November 14, 1969, as Apollo 12 was lifting off from its launchpad in Cape Canaveral, Florida, it was struck by lightning. Twice. First at 36.5 seconds after liftoff and then again at 52 seconds. Later the incident reports would show that the lightning had caused a power surge and inadvertently disconnected the fuel cells, leading to a voltage drop.

In the moment though, there was anything but clarity.

In an instant, every alarm in the Apollo 12 command capsule went off. Telemetry readings in Houston were complete gibberish. For an organization that thinks through everything, they never thought to ask what to do when lightning strikes. What were the chances?

Even worse, the stakes couldn't be higher. If the mission is aborted, NASA loses a $1.2 billion rocket. If not, and the safety of the astronauts is compromised, you end up broadcasting a catastrophe to the whole world. When listening back to a recording of mission control, you can feel the tension and stress.

There's a moment of silence on the audio loop before someone cuts in: "try SCE to Aux." This wasn't something ever tried before. So much so, someone radios back "what the hell is that?" With no better options, the command is relayed to the astronauts. And it worked. After searching for the switch, they flip it, and everything immediately returns back to normal.

The NASA engineer John Aaron gave the obscure suggestion. A year earlier he'd been working in an Apollo capsule simulator and ended up with a similar mess of telemetry readings. Rather than reset the simulator, he decided to play around and try fixing the problem. He'd discover that by shifting the signal conditioning electronics, or SCE, system to its auxiliary setting, it could operate in low-voltage conditions, restoring telemetry. SCE to Aux.

The lightning strike was a black swan event, something NASA had never simulated before. What inspired John Aaron to dig around to uncover the cause of that specific data signature? In an oral history with NASA (*https://oreil.ly/xDv75*), he credits a "natural curiosity with why things work and how they work."

Curiosity is a trait found in many SREs. We were reminded of a conversation with an SRE friend in Dublin who shared how she was the type to keep asking why about the systems she worked with. That echoes John Aaron talking about how he always wanted to know how things around him worked, and not stopping until he had a deep understanding.

That willingness to learn makes sense for SREs, given the need to work with complex systems. The systems change constantly, and the role requires someone wanting to ask questions about how they work. The inquisitivity means rather than seeing one specific part of the system as their domain, SREs instead wonder about all the parts of the system, and how they function together.

But it's not just the technical system. SREs need to be curious about people too, the socio- part of the sociotechnical system. Without that, you couldn't bring different teams together to create meaningful SLOs. You couldn't navigate personality types to properly respond to incidents. You'd be satisfied with just the five whys and miss out on uncovering the lessons to be learned post-incident.

We want this book to give you an opportunity to explore, play, and satisfy your curiosity. Here, we've laid out essays to do so. (You may notice there are actually 98 essays! We figured everyone likes a little something extra on the house.) They're written by experts from across the industry, guiding you through a range of topics from the fundamentals of SRE to the bleeding edge. This book was written and edited during the pandemic, and we are deeply grateful for everyone who contributed during such a trying time.

We believe that SRE needs to be filled with many voices, and that new voices should always be welcome. New ideas from different points of view and a wide range of experiences will help evolve this field that is, honestly, remarkably still in its early days. Our dream is that as you read these essays, they spark your curiosity, and move you forward in your SRE journey, no matter where you're currently at.

We're beyond curious to read what a batch of essays on SRE will look like in 5 or 10 years.

How We Structured the Book

SRE, although it deals with complex technical systems, is ultimately a cultural practice. Culture is the product of people, and that inspired us to organize this book into sections based on the number of SREs you have in your organization—what you specifically tackle and how your day looks like depends on how many SREs there are. We've broken the book's essays into "New to SRE," 0-1 SRE, 1-10 SREs, 10-100 SREs, and the "Future of SRE."

Readers looking for guidance on where to start first can jump right to the section that applies most to them; however, you will still find value in reading essays from sections that don't currently apply to your day-to-day.

At 0 to 1 SRE, no one has been designated an SRE yet, or you have found your very first one, a role that can seem almost lonely.

At 1 to 10 SREs, you are forming a team, and there is sharing of knowledge and the ability to divvy up work.

At 10 to 100 SREs, you have become an organization, and you need to think not just about the systems you're working on, but also about how you organize that many SREs.

"New to SRE" covers foundational topics (although not exhaustively!) and is helpful both for those just starting their SRE journeys as well as a refresher for even the most seasoned SRE. "Future of SRE" contains essays that look into where SRE is potentially headed, or are (for the moment) sitting on the zeitgeist.

There's no need to read the book in any particular order. You can read it from cover to cover. Or, if you are curious about a particular topic, flip to the index where you can find all the essays on that topic. Use this as a reference guide, or a source of inspiration—one that can provide a jolt as needed. Or, maybe create a reading club, where once a week you pick an essay to discuss with your coworkers. This is the beauty of a collection of essays. We hope you enjoy reading them as much as we did.

O'Reilly Online Learning

O'REILLY® For more than 40 years, *O'Reilly Media* has provided technology and business training, knowledge, and insight to help companies succeed.

Our unique network of experts and innovators share their knowledge and expertise through books, articles, and our online learning platform. O'Reilly's online learning platform gives you on-demand access to live training courses, in-depth learning paths, interactive coding environments, and a vast collection of text and video from O'Reilly and 200+ other publishers. For more information, visit *http://oreilly.com*.

How to Contact Us

Please address comments and questions concerning this book to the publisher:

O'Reilly Media, Inc.
1005 Gravenstein Highway North
Sebastopol, CA 95472
800-998-9938 (in the United States or Canada)
707-829-0515 (international or local)
707-829-0104 (fax)

We have a web page for this book, where we list errata, examples, and any additional information. You can access this page at *https://oreil.ly/97-SRE*.

Email *bookquestions@oreilly.com* to comment or ask technical questions about this book.

Visit *http://oreilly.com* for news and information about our courses and books.

Find us on Facebook: *http://facebook.com/oreilly*

Follow us on Twitter: *http://twitter.com/oreillymedia*

Watch us on YouTube: *http://youtube.com/oreillymedia*

Acknowledgments

Writing a book makes you acutely aware of the passage of time—even more so during a pandemic. During tumultuous times, you realize how important the people in your lives are. Some we can't hug until this pandemic is over. Others we won't be able to hug even after then. We hold dear thoughts of our loved ones here and beyond.

PART I

New to SRE

Site Reliability Engineering in Six Words

Alex Hidalgo

Nobl9

When someone I've just met asks me what I do for a living, I generally fall back to something along the lines of, "I'm a site reliability engineer. We keep large-scale computer services reliable." For many people, this is sufficiently boring and our general pleasantries continue. Occasionally, though, I run into people who are a bit more curious than that: "Oh, that sounds interesting! How do you do that?"

That's a difficult question to answer! What do SREs actually *do*? For many years, I'd rely on just listing an assortment of things—some of which have made their way into essays in this very book. Although an answer like that wasn't exactly *wrong*, it also never felt truly satisfying. There had to be a more cohesive answer, and when I reflect on my decade of performing this job, I think I've finally figured it out. Virtually everything SREs do relies on our ability to do six things: measure, analyze, decide, act, reflect, and repeat.

Measuring does not just mean collecting data. To *measure* something, you have some sort of goal in mind. You don't *collect* flour to bake a cake, you *measure* the flour; otherwise, things will end up a mess. SREs need to measure things because pure data isn't enough. Our data needs to be meaningful. We need to be able to answer the question, "Is this service doing what its users need it to be doing?"

Once you have measurements, the next step is to analyze them. This is when some basic statistics and probability analysis can be helpful. Learn as much as you can from the things you are measuring by using the centuries of study and knowledge mathematicians have made available to us.

Now you've done your best at measuring and analyzing how a certain thing is behaving. Use this analysis to make a decision about how best to move into the future!

Then you must act. You actually need to do the thing you decided to do. It could be that this action is actually to take no action at all!

Finally, reflect on what you did once you've done it. Place a critical—but blameless—eye squarely on whatever you've done. You can generally learn much more from this process than you can from your initial measurement analysis.

Now you start over. Something has either changed about the world due to your decision or it hasn't, and you need to keep measuring to see what the real impact of this action, or inaction, actually was. Keep measuring and then analyze, decide, act, reflect, and repeat again and again. It's the SRE way. Incremental progress is the only reliable way to reliability.

Site reliability engineering is a broad discipline. We are often called on to be software engineers, system administrators, network engineers, systems architects, and even educators or consultants, but one paradigm that flows through all of those roles is that SRE is data-driven. Measure the things you need to measure, analyze the data you collect, decide what to do with this analysis, act on your findings, reflect on your decision, and then do it all over, again and again and again.

Measure, analyze, decide, act, reflect and repeat: that's site reliability engineering in six words.

Do We Know Why We Really Want Reliability?

Niall Murphy

Microsoft

Do we really understand reliability, or why we would want it?

This may seem like a strange question. It is an article of faith in this community that unreachable online services have no value (*https://oreil.ly/sk4A_*). But even a moment's thought will show you that's simply not true. You yourself encounter intermittent computer failure almost every day. Some contexts even seem to expect it; with web services, users are highly accustomed to hitting refresh or (for more difficult problems) clearing cookies, restarting a browser, or restarting a machine. Even services themselves have retry protocols.

A certain amount of fudge is baked into every human–computer interaction. Even for longer outages, people almost always come back if you're down for a few minutes, and have even more patience, depending on the uniqueness of the service provided.

It's anecdotal, but suggestive: I had a conversation with a very well-known company a couple of years ago when they said they didn't put any money into reliability because their particular customer base had nowhere else to go. Therefore, time they spent on reliability would be time they wouldn't spend on capturing revenue; it wasn't worth it.

I gasped inwardly at the time, but I've thought about it often since, and I turn the question toward us, as a community, now: do we have any *real* argument against that statement, as a community and a profession? Can we put any numbers around it? Understand what the trade-offs are? Make anything other than emotive claims about brand image? Come up with a *real* explanation of why companies previously lambasted for their unreliability (*http://twitter.com*) are worth tens of billions today (*https://oreil.ly/lHuMO*), never mind companies where the inability to access the site costs real money (*https://oreil.ly/Ak3rc*), outages frequently last hours, yet usage, revenue, and profits keep going up (*https://oreil.ly/opYsE*)?

I don't like it, but I think it's true; in a rising market, if a company could choose to acquire new customers or retain existing ones, every economic incentive is toward customer acquisition, since each customer lost would be replaced by many more gained. Of course, a systematically unreliable platform would *eventually* lose you as many customers as you acquired, but you have time to fix that, and customers are often reluctant to change, even given poor service.

Product developers know this, and this is why our conversations are so fraught. Yet we don't have a fully satisfactory way to talk about these trade-offs today; the true value of reliability, particularly for markets that are not rising, non-web contexts, or other areas where SREs are not commonly found, is hard to articulate. The SLO model, which is meant to be able to articulate the nuances of precisely how much unreliability a given customer base can tolerate in the aggregate, is not actually sufficient; as typically used, it cannot distinguish between (say) 20 minutes of almost complete unavailability or two hours of intermittent unavailability. These situations are actually very different from the customer experience point of view and, potentially, also from the revenue generation point of view.

We have sparse data points (*https://oreil.ly/TlBTu*) that tenuously suggest the outlines of an approach that would enable us to understand, and argue successfully for why to spend time on reliability in the face of limited time and resources—or even worse, in a rising market—but we are very far from understanding it all.

This is therefore, depending on your point of view, quite worrying or a wonderful opportunity to stop spending a lot of time and money.

Building Self-Regulating Processes

Denise Yu

GitHub

In Camille Fournier's excellent book, *The Manager's Path* (*https://oreil.ly/ Bhs1O*) (O'Reilly, 2017), she advises readers to look for "self-regulating processes," which caught my eye. My undergraduate degree is in economics, and I jump at any opportunity to apply economic thinking to practical problem-solving. Self-regulating processes are tiny cycles of checks and balances, and it's cool to find them in human systems.

In my tech network, I often hear about process experiments succeeding or failing by the emotional or political bandwidth of the person who initiated the experiment. For example, when introducing pair-programming to a new group of engineers, it often takes a confident, charismatic person to coax reluctant teammates to start pairing for the first time.

In fact, they might not even call it pairing to begin with—they'll say, "Hey, do you wanna come over here and have a look at this with me?" But when that person leaves a company, pairing might fall by the wayside, because it was something driven by the strength of a personality. These short-lived process innovations are valuable, but they don't last; so in that context, we never learn how to adjust them, measure them, and scale them.

Self-regulating processes, on the other hand, don't depend on strong personalities to persist. The way that they work is by aligning incentives (both the positive and negative kind) in such a way that no one person is stuck with the unpleasant task of hassling other people to do their parts. Micromanagement represents exactly the opposite outcome of a self-regulating process.

To understand how to align incentives, let's talk about what incentives *are*. *Positive incentives* represent net gains for an individual if they behave in a certain manner. Think carrots, not sticks. They come in many flavors: financial (e.g., wages, stock awards), social (e.g., peer recognition), or intrinsic (e.g., mastery of a particular skill), to name a few.

Most people are driven by the positive incentive of wanting to earn more money, and perhaps wanting a better title. To facilitate that, most people, given that the organization exhibits more of a generative culture (*https://oreil.ly/T5Tpd*), would agree that receiving honest and constructive feedback from their peers is a good way to improve their performance.

Negative incentives are the opposite: net losses. Similarly, most people react to a set of negative incentives, such as wanting to avoid negative social repercussions and unnecessarily spending social capital. Consider that at companies with unlimited vacation policies (*https://oreil.ly/-TpHv*), people end up taking fewer vacation days than their peers who accrue fixed vacation throughout the year. This is because a financial incentive structure became replaced by a social incentive structure, and the social anti-incentives feel more costly, in part because they're really hard to quantify, and we're wired to dislike uncertainty.

A self-regulating process sets up the right combination of positive incentives and negative incentives, so that people are intrinsically motivated to follow the process, and no external encouragement or facilitation is necessarily required once things get underway. Balancing positive with negative incentives is important: too much negativity and people will start to feel fearful; too much positivity and you bank on the assumption that everyone feels equally motivated by the same carrots. (That often is not true.)

In software engineering companies, and probably in other companies as well, I believe that you can design self-regulating processes if you stop and think about what incentives are in play.

Four Engineers of an SRE Seder

Jacob Scott

Stripe

During Seder, families recite a passage addressing the questions one might ask about the Passover holiday. The questions, presented from the points of view of four children, help pass the importance of the holiday down the generations. Here I present four software engineers asking about the importance of reliability.

The selfish engineer asks, "Why is your reliability so poor?" By using the word *your* and not *our*, the selfish engineer disclaims responsibility for reliability. Life is certainly easier when reliability is *your* job, not *our* job—but reliability is more and more frequently a collective responsibility.

To him, we must explain the importance, both to himself and to his team, of owning his code in production. As he decides what sort of observability to add to his features, which queries to make to data stores, or whether to push back on a resource-intensive feature request, this engineer—like every other—affects the behavior and reliability of production. None of us can avoid this power over production, and if we avoid responsibility for it, we implicitly place that burden on others. Given the importance and inevitability of this responsibility, we ask him to consider whether he might find more career growth and success in embracing responsibility than shirking it.

The junior engineer asks, "It works on my machine. Why isn't that enough?" If only success in development environments implied success in production! To him, we sketch the vast difference between development and production. We might compare the scale and complexity of data in production to the limited, curated snapshot optimized for development. Or, we might contrast the sophisticated networking topology configured in production with the local and stubbed services in development that help him test and iterate quickly.

We suggest this engineer review a few of the spiciest or most mind-melting incident reports in our archive. Among the contributing factors whose confluence spawned these incidents, a few would certainly never show up (let alone reproducibly!) in a development environment.

The wise engineer, having responded to many incidents and read widely, asks, "How can error budgets prevent my next serious incident?" The oh-so-unfortunate truth is that error budgets are retrospective and cannot predict—let alone prevent—incidents.

To her, we note that although error budgets can't predict or prevent incidents, they provide a foundation for *preparing* for incidents. The process of defining error budgets creates alignment, transparency, and common ground about what reliability means, not just to engineers and users but also to executives, sales and marketing, front-line support, and the organization writ large.

We ask her to be curious about her error budgets and to reflect on what she learns about our users' desires for our system. Does she find that error budgets help elicit an active and ongoing discussion about the behavior of production? Over the long haul, this helps reduce the likelihood and impact of incidents.

Finally, the engineer who isn't sure how to frame their question asks, "Why is reliability important? Why should we be curious and passionate about it?" To them, we state that reliability is about systems behaving as expected, and users want software to be reliable! Availability—responding quickly and correctly to requests or, colloquially, not failing—is one common example. Users also want software to change and improve, often in the form of new features, better performance, or reduction in cost.

These desires are frequently in tension with each other, and he should reflect on SRE as an approach to quantifying reliability to help our entire organization understand the trade-offs involved.

The Reliability Stack

Alex Hidalgo

Nobl9

Think about your favorite digital media streaming service. You've settled down on the couch to watch a movie and you click a button on your remote. Most of the time, the movie buffers for a few seconds and then starts playing.

But what if the movie takes a full 20 seconds to buffer? You'd probably be a little annoyed in the moment, but ultimately, the rest of the movie streams just fine. Even with this little bit of failure, this service has still acted reliably for you, since the majority of the time it doesn't take anywhere near 20 seconds.

What happens if it takes 20 seconds to buffer every single time? Now things go from momentarily annoying to fully unreliable. With the plethora of digital media streaming services available, you might choose to abandon this service and switch to a different one.

Nothing is ever perfect and nothing can ever be 100% reliable. This is not only the way of the world, it also turns out that people are totally fine with this! No one actually expects computer systems to run perfectly all the time; we just need them to be reliable enough often enough.

How do we figure out the right level of reliability? This is where the reliability stack comes into play. It's made up of three components: SLIs (service level indicators), SLOs (service level objectives), and error budgets.

At the base of the reliability stack are SLIs, which are measurements of your service from your users' point of view. Why users? Because that's who your system has to perform well for. Your users determine whether you're being reliable. No user cares whether things look good from your end if their movies take 20 seconds to buffer every single time. An example SLI might be, "Movies buffer for 5 seconds or less."

Next are SLOs themselves. SLOs are fueled by SLIs. If SLIs are measurements about how your service is operating, SLOs are targets for how often you want them to be operating well enough. Using our example, you might now want to say something like, "Movies buffer for 5 seconds or less 99% of the time."

If buffer times exceed 5 seconds only once in 100 times, people will probably be okay with this.

Nothing is ever perfect, so don't aim for it. Ensure instead that you're aiming to be reliable just enough of the time. You'll spend an infinite number of resources—both financial and human—trying to aim for perfection.

Finally, at the top of the reliability stack are error budgets, which are informed by SLOs and are simply a measurement of how you've performed against your target over a period of time. It's much more useful to know how you've performed from your users' perspective over a week, a month, or a quarter than simply knowing how you're performing right now. An error budget lets you say things like, "We cannot buffer reliably for 7 hours, 18 minutes, and 17 seconds every 30 days." You can use error budgets to think more holistically about the reliability of your service. Use this data to have better discussions and make better decisions about addressing reliability concerns.

You can't be perfect, and it turns out no one expects you to be perfect anyway. Use the reliability stack to ensure that you're being reliable *enough*.

Infrastructure: It's Where the Power Is

Charity Majors

Honeycomb.io

"Why infrastructure, why ops?" a coworker asked me, years ago. It was a software engineer, after a particularly gnarly on-call rotation, and the subtext was crystal clear: was I tricked into making this career choice—the sacrifice of being tethered to a pager, the pressure of being the debugger of last resort? Who would ever choose this life?

Without missing a beat, I answered: "Because that's where the power is." Then I stopped in surprise, hearing what I had said. We aren't used to thinking of infra as a powerful role. CS (computer science) departments, the media, and the popular imagination all revolve around algorithms and data structures, the heroic writer of code and shipper of features.

To business people, operations is a cost center, an unfortunate necessity. This is a historical artifact; operations should be seen as yin to development's yang, united and inseparable, never "someone else's job." Biz is the why, dev is the what, and ops is the how. Whether your company has one person or one thousand.

Code is ephemeral. Features come and go. Crafting a product in a modern development environment feels to me like erecting cloud castles in the sky: abstractions atop other abstractions, building up this rich mental world in your mind.

Software engineers are modern magicians, crafting unthinkably complex spells and incantations that spin gold from straw, generating immense real value practically out of thin air. But what happens when those spells go wrong?

A couple of years into my first job as a sysadmin, I started to notice a pattern when very senior engineers would come to me and the other ops people. They understood their code far better than I did, but when it stopped working in production, they would panic. Why didn't it work like it did yesterday?

What changed? It was as though production were a foreign land, and they needed me to accompany them as a translator.

I always had crushes on the people who could turn "it's slow" into "the query planner is doing multiple full-table scans because it is using the wrong compound index." Any of us could see that it was slow; explaining *why* was next-level interesting.

Software can seem as mysterious and arcane as any ritual of the occult, but infrastructure engineers have a grimoire of tools to inspect the ritual relentlessly from every possible angle. Trace the library calls, scan the ports, step through the system calls, dump the packets.

Infrastructure tools remind us that software operates according to the laws of scientific realism. Every mystery will yield an answer if pursued with enough persistence. To do so requires a world-weary fearlessness when things go wrong. The harder and more subtle the bug, the more interested and energized they become. Infra engineers have never seen an abstraction we trust to work as designed. The grander the claim, the more pessimistic we become.

We aren't so much cynical as we are grimly certain that everything will fail, and it will fall to us to save the world with nothing but a paper clip and a soldering iron. We compulsively peek under the lid to see what horrifying things are being done in the name of monkey patching.

When we get together with other infrastructure engineers over a pint, we boast about the outages we have seen, the bugs we have found, and the you-won't-believe-what-happened-last-holiday stories.

There is power in knowing how to be self-sufficient, in having the tools and the fearlessness, to track the answer down through layer after layer of abstractions. At the base of every technical pile sits the speed of light, which cannot be messed with or mocked up.

Thinking About Resilience

Justin Li

Shopify

In resilient systems, important variables stay in their desired state even when other variables leave their normal state. For example, many animals are able to avoid dying from minor cuts. When skin is cut, unprotected blood-carrying tissue is exposed, yet blood loss quickly trends back to zero as a clot forms. Improving a system's resilience makes dependent variables describing that system more independent.

Networked systems are often required to respond quickly, expressed as a state like this: *99th percentile latency below one second*. Ideally, this is held true all the way to the required limits of the system, for instance, *1s peak request rate of 100000 per second*. We want to ensure that the *latency* variable isn't too dependent on the *request rate* variable.

Here are ways we improve resilience:

Load reduction
Throttling, load shedding/prioritization, queuing, load balancing

Latency reduction
Caching, regional replication

Load adaptation
Autoscaling, overprovisioning

Resilience (specifically)
Timeouts, circuit breakers, bulkheads, retries, failovers, fallbacks

Meta-techniques
Improving tooling, perhaps to scale up or fail over faster; especially impactful in cases when slow humans are in a system's critical path

Some of these tools are not usually associated with resilience (they are general optimization techniques), but all influence the dependence of critical variables. Sometimes they interact in useful ways. For example, retries can correct for transient downtime caused by a failover.

These tools also recur at multiple layers. TCP retransmission works against packet loss, but application-level retries are also used, because TCP can't retry an entire stream (among other reasons).

Let's continue the latency example. In practice, the relationship between request rate and latency is not linear but usually follows some rational function. Until a certain load is reached, the system is unsaturated and can respond quickly, but when load approaches capacity, queues quickly fill up and latency grows accordingly.

We can scale the system by adding servers, which stretches the function horizontally, allowing more requests to be served before violating the latency objective. This costs money. If we don't like that, we can look at other options, such as load shedding: drop work (limit *request rate*) when the system is overloaded (*latency* reaches its limit).

Errors have a monetary impact too, but it might be less than paying for more servers if this condition is rare enough. The cost can be reduced further by dropping unimportant work first. Most important, the load-shedding approach entirely prevents unbounded latency growth, avoiding potential cascading failure.

You can think about every resilience tool as illustrated below:

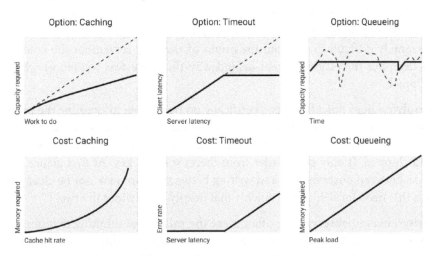

By building in resilience, we can help increase reliability so the system bounces back and continues to function under adverse conditions.

Observability in the Development Cycle

Charity Majors and Liz Fong-Jones

Honeycomb.io

Catching bugs cleanly, resolving them swiftly, and preventing them from becoming a backlog of technical debt that weighs down the development process relies on a team's ability to find those bugs quickly. Yet software development teams often hinder their ability to do so for a variety of reasons.

Consider organizations where software engineers aren't responsible for operating their software in production. Engineers merge their code into master, cross their fingers that this change won't be one that breaks prod, and wait to get paged if a problem occurs. Sometimes they get paged soon after deployment. The deployment is then rolled back and the triggering changes can be examined for bugs. More likely, problems wouldn't be detected for hours, days, weeks, or months after that code had been merged. By that time, it's extremely difficult to pick out the origin of the bug, remember the context, or decipher the original intent behind why that code was written or why it shipped.

Resolving bugs quickly depends critically on being able to examine the problem *while the original intent is still fresh in the original author's head*. It will never again be as easy to debug a problem as it was right after it was written and shipped. It only gets harder from there; speed is key. At first glance, the links between observability and writing better software may not be clear, but it is this need for debugging quickly that deeply intertwines the two.

Newcomers to observability often make the mistake of thinking that observability is a way to debug your code, similar to using highly verbose logging. Although it's possible to debug your code, using observability tools, that is not the primary purpose of observability. Observability operates on the order of *systems*, not on the order of *functions*. Emitting enough detail at the lines level to debug code reliably would emit so much output that it would swamp most observability systems with an obscene amount of storage and scale. It would simply be impractical to pay for a system capable of doing that because it would likely cost somewhere in the ballpark of 1X–10X as much as your system itself.

Observability is not for debugging your code logic. *Observability is for figuring out where in your systems to find the code you need to debug.* Observability tools help you narrow down swiftly where problems may be occurring. From which component did an error originate? Where is latency being introduced? Where was a piece of this data munged? Which hop is taking up the most processing time? Is that wait time evenly distributed across all users, or is it only experienced by a subset thereof? Observability helps your investigation of problems pinpoint likely sources.

Often, observability will also give you a good idea of what might be happening in or around an affected component or what the bug might be, or even provide hints to where the bug is actually happening—your code, the platform's code, or a higher-level architectural object.

Once you've identified where the bug lives and some qualities about how it arises, observability's job is done. If you want to dive deeper into the code itself, the tool you want is a debugger (for example, gdb). Once you suspect how to reproduce the problem, you can spin up a local instance of the code, copy over the full context from the service, and continue your investigation. Though related, the difference between an observability tool and a debugger is an order of scale; like a telescope and a microscope, they are primarily designed for different things.

> Adapted from the upcoming book *Observability Engineering*, expected in 2021 from O'Reilly.

There Is No Magic

Bouke van der Bijl

When working with computers it's easy to get overwhelmed with the complexity of it all. You write some code, run it through a compiler, and execute it on your machine. It seems like magic.

But when issues occur and things break down, it's important to remember that there is no magic. These systems we work with are designed and built by humans like you, and that means that they can also be understood by humans like you. At every step, from the interface on the screen to the atoms your processor is built out of, someone considered how things should work.

I tend to work on two layers at the same time: the code I'm writing and the lower-level code I'm using. I switch back and forth between my work in progress and the source code of the Ruby gem, the Go compiler, or even a disassembly if the source is not available. This gives me context about my dependency: are there comments explaining weird behavior? Should I be using a different function mentioned in the code? Maybe an argument that wasn't immediately clear from the docs, or even a glaring bug?

I find this context switching to be a sort of superpower: X-ray goggles for the software developer. You can look deeper many times: from your code, to the virtual machine running it, to the C language it's written in, to the assembly that finally runs. Even then, you can read the Intel x86 manual to try to figure out what happens in the machine and how the various instructions are encoded. Software systems are fractal in nature—every component a world in itself.

Of course, just because all these things are created by people like us doesn't mean that it's possible for one person to understand it all. We stand on the shoulders of thousands of giants, and millennia of hours have been put into the systems to get where we are today.

It would take many lifetimes to know deeply every single step from atoms to GUIs, and that can be intimidating, but it doesn't mean we shouldn't try.

When you assume that the components we build our software from are mysterious scriptures that you can't understand or change, you will make uninformed decisions that don't account for the actual situation. Instead, you need to be more clear-eyed. You need to work with the quirks of the underlying system and use them to your advantage instead of paving over them.

So next time a library you use does something unexpected, take that extra step and pop open the hood. Poke and prod at the internals, look around, and make some changes. You will end up pleasantly surprised finding whole new worlds to explore and improve.

How Wikipedia Is Served to You

Effie Mouzeli

Wikimedia Foundation

According to Wikipedia, "Wikipedia is a multilingual, web-based, free-content encyclopedia project supported by the Wikimedia Foundation and based on a model of openly editable content." Serving billions of page views per month, Wikipedia is one of highest-traffic websites in the world. Let me explain what happens when you are visiting Wikipedia to read about Saint Helena or llamas.

First, these are the three most important building blocks of our infrastructure:

- The CDN (content delivery network), which is our caching layer
- The application layer
- Open-source software

When you request a page, the magic of our geographic DNS and internet routing sends this request to the nearest Wikimedia data center, based on your location, while with the wizardry of TLS, ATS (Apache Traffic Server) encrypts your connection. Each data center has two caching layers: in-memory (Varnish) and on disk (ATS). Most requests terminate here, because the hottest URLs are always cached. In case of cache misses, the request will be forwarded to the application layer, which might be very near if this is a primary data center, or a bit farther away if this is a caching point.

Our application layer has MediaWiki (*https://www.mediawiki.org*) at its core, supported by a number of microservices and databases. MediaWiki is an Apache, PHP, MySQL open-source application, developed for Wikipedia. MediaWiki will look for a rendered version of the article initially on Memcached and, if not found, then on a MariaDB database cluster called Parser Cache.

If MediaWiki gets misses from Memcached and Parser Cache, it will pull the article's Wikitext (*https://oreil.ly/nA9TI*) and render it. Articles are stored in two database clusters: the Wikitext cluster, where Wikitext is stored in blobs, and the metadata cluster, which tells MediaWiki where an article is located in the Wikitext cluster. After an article is rendered, it is stored in turn in all aforementioned caches and, of course, is served back to you.

Things are slightly simpler when the request is a media file rather than a page. On a cache miss in the caching layer, ATS will directly fetch the file from Swift, a scalable object storage system by OpenStack.

As you can see, MediaWiki is surrounded by a very thick caching layer, and the reason is simple: rendering pages is costly. Furthermore, when a page is edited, it needs to be invalidated from all these caches and then populated again. When very famous people die, our infrastructure experiences a phenomenon called celebrity death spikes (or the Michael Jackson effect [1]). During this event, everyone links to Wikipedia to read about them while editors are spiking the edit rate by constantly updating the person's article. Eventually, this could cause noticeable load as heavy read traffic focuses on an article that's constantly being invalidated from caches.

The final building block is our use of open-source software. Everything we run in our infrastructure is open source, including in-house developed applications and tools. The community around the Wikimedia movement (*https://oreil.ly/MoBll*) is not only limited to caring for the content in the various projects, its contribution extends to the software and systems serving it. Open source made it possible for members of the community to contribute; it is an integral part of Wikipedia and one of the driving forces behind our technical choices. Wikipedia obeys Conway's law (*https://oreil.ly/0PXjw*) in a way: a website that promotes access to free knowledge runs on free software.

It might sound surprising that one of the most popular websites is run using only open-source software and without an army of engineers—but this is Wikipedia; openness is part of its existence.

---

1 Thomas Steiner, Seth Hooland, and Ed Summers. (2013). MJ no more: Using concurrent Wikipedia edit spikes with social network plausibility checks for breaking news detection, 791–794. 10.1145/2487788.2488049.

Why You Should Understand (a Little) About TCP

Julia Evans

Wizard Zines

I'd like to convince you that understanding a little bit about TCP (like how packets work and what an ACK is) is important, even if you only have systems that are making regular boring HTTP requests. Let's start with a mystery I ran into at work: the case of the extra 40 milliseconds.

One day, someone mentioned in Slack, "Hey, I'm publishing messages to NSQ and it's taking 40 ms each time." A little background: NSQ is a queue. The way you publish a message is to make an HTTP request on localhost. It really should not take 40 *milliseconds* to send an HTTP request to localhost. Something was terribly wrong. The NSQ daemon wasn't under high CPU load, it wasn't using a lot of memory, it didn't seem to be in a garbage collection pause. Help!

Then I remembered an article I'd read a week before, called, "In Search of Performance: How We Shaved 200 ms Off Every POST Request." That article described how the combination of two TCP features (delayed ACKs and Nagle's algorithm) conspired to add a lot of extra time to every POST request.

Here's how delayed ACKs plus Nagle's algorithm can make your HTTP requests slow. I'll tell you what was happening in the blog post I read. First, some background about their setup:

- They had an application making requests to HAProxy.
- Their HTTP library (Ruby's Net::HTTP) was sending POST requests in two small packets (one for the headers and one for the body).

Here's what the TCP exchange looked like:

1. client: hi! here's packet 1.
2. server: <silence>. ("I'll ACK eventually but let's just wait for the second packet.")
3. client: <silence>. ("I have more data to send but let's wait for the ACK.")
4. server: ok i'm bored. here's an ACK.
5. client: great here's the second packet!!!

That period while the client and server are both passive-aggressively waiting for the other to send information? That's the extra 200 ms! The client was waiting because of Nagle's algorithm, and the server was waiting because of delayed ACKs.

Delayed ACKs and Nagle's algorithm are both enabled by default on Linux, so this isn't that unusual. If you send your data in more than one TCP packet, it can happen to you.

The solution is TCP_NODELAY. When I read this article, I thought, "That can't be my problem, can it? Can it? The problem can't be with TCP!" But I'd read that you could fix this by enabling TCP_NODELAY on the client, a socket option that disables Nagle's algorithm, and that seemed easy to test, so I committed a change, turning on TCP_NODELAY for our application, and BOOM. All of the 40 ms delays instantly disappeared. Everything was fixed. I was a wizard.

You can't fix TCP problems without understanding TCP. I used to think that TCP was really low-level and that I did not need to understand it—which is mostly true! But sometimes in real life, you have a bug, and that bug is because of something in the TCP algorithm. I've found that in operations work, a surprising number of these bugs are caused by a low-level component of my system that I previously thought was obscure and suddenly have to learn a *lot* more about very quickly.

The reason I was able to understand and fix this bug is that, two years earlier, I'd spent a week writing a toy TCP stack in Python to learn how TCP works. Having a basic understanding of the TCP protocol and how packets are ACKed really helped me work through this problem.

The Importance of a Management Interface

Salim Virji

Google

During an outage, you care more about being able to control the system than about the system answering all user-facing requests. By adapting the concept of a *control plane* from networking hardware, engineers can separate responsibility for data transmission from control messages. The control plane provides a uniform point of entry for administrative and operational tasks, distinct from sending user data itself. For reliability purposes, this separation provides a way for operators to manage a system even when it is not functioning as expected. Let's look at why this is important and how you know when to separate these parts of a system.

In an early version of the GFS (Google File System), a single designated node was responsible for all data lookups: each of the thousands of clients began their request for data by asking this single node for the canonical location. This single node was also responsible for responding to administrative requests such as, "How many data requests are in the queue right now?" The same process was responsible for these two sets of requests—one user-facing and critical and the other strictly internal and also critical—and the process served responses to both from the same thread pool. This meant that when the server was overloaded and unable to process incoming requests, the SREs responsible for the system were unable to send administrative requests to lighten the load!

Previous versions of GFS had never been overloaded in this way due to client demand, which was why the request contention had not been apparent. In the next version, we separated the resources responsible for operations in the critical path from resources for administrative action using a control plane, and GFS production quality was able to take a significant step forward.

By extending this notion across multiple services, the benefits of a single administrative programming interface become apparent: software for automation can send an "update to new version" instruction to a heterogeneous group of servers, and they can interpret it and act accordingly. By dropping the networking nomenclature, we separate our requests into a *management* layer and a *data* layer and see the importance of separating the two for any service in the critical path. By drawing a boundary between user-facing operations, we can also have more confidence in the instrumentation we apply to the data measurements; operations in the data layer will use and measure resources in that layer and not mingle with operations in the management layer. This in turn leads to a more successful approach to measuring user-facing operations, a useful metric for service level objectives.

How do you know when you have properly isolated administrative requests from user requests? Tools such as OpenTracing might show the full path of a management call as well as a user request, possibly exposing unintended interactions. Indeed, your systems will likely have connection points such as where the management interface actually influences user paths. Although the separation is not total and absolute, an SRE should be able to identify the boundaries between these parts of the systems they build and operate.

To implement this separation for software that's already built, such as third-party applications, you may need to add a separate service that, like a sidecar, attaches to the core software and, through a common interface such as an HTTP server, provides an endpoint for the administrative API. This glued-on management layer may be the precursor to eventual integration with the core software, or it might be a long-term solution. This approach to system design separates the request paths servicing user-facing requests from the requests providing management responsibility.

When It Comes to Storage, Think Distributed

Salim Virji

Google

Almost every application, whether on a smartphone or running in a web browser, generates and stores data. As SREs, we often have the responsibility for managing the masses of information that guide and inform decisions for applications as wide-ranging as thermostats to traffic-routing to sharing cat pictures. Distributed storage systems have gained popularity because they provide fault-tolerant and reliable approaches to data management and offer a scalable approach to data storage and retrieval.

Distributed storage is distinct from storage appliances, storage arrays, and storage physically attached to the computer using it; distributed storage systems decouple data producers from the physical media that store this data. By spreading the risk of data storage across different physical media, the system provides *speed* and *reliability,* two features that are fundamental to providing a good user experience, whether your user is a human excitedly sharing photographs with family and friends around the world or another computer processing data in a pipeline.

Distributed storage enables concurrent client access: as the system writes the data to multiple locations, there's no single disk head to block all read operations. Additional copies of the data can be made asynchronously to support increased read demand from clients if the data becomes really hot, such as a popular video. This is an example of the horizontal scaling made possible by a distributed system; although RAID (redundant array of independent disks) systems keep multiple copies of the data, they are not available for concurrent client reads in this same way.

As an additional benefit, building applications on top of distributed storage systems means that organizations don't have to post "Our service will be unavailable tonight from 3–4 for scheduled maintenance" while operators apply a kernel patch or other critical upgrade to the storage device. There is no single storage device; there is a storage *system*, with replication and redundancy.

The promise of modern web services, a *globally consistent* view of data, whether for a single user or for a large organization, would be almost impossible to implement without distributed storage systems. Previously, this required expensive device-to-device synchronization, essentially copying disks or directory trees from one specific computer to another; each was a single point of failure (SPOF).

Fault tolerance forms a key part of reliability; by sharing risk across different devices, distributed storage systems tolerate faults that storage appliances cannot. Although storage appliances might have multiple local power modules, distributed storage systems have similar power redundancy plus rack-level power diversity. This further dilutes risk and, when the distributed storage system uses this diversity to refine data placement, will result in data storage resilience to many levels of power failure.

SREs responsible for distributed storage systems need to pay attention to different metrics than they do for a single network-attached storage device. For example, they will monitor the computed recoverability of discrete chunks of data. This involves understanding the system's implementation: how does the storage system lay out the data, and where does it replicate the constituent data parts? How often does the system need to recopy data to maintain *risk diversity*, an indicator of how accurately it will be able to retrieve data? How often does the system metadata have a cache miss, causing longer data-retrieval times?

As distributed storage systems enable applications used around the globe and with massive quantities of data, they present observability opportunities for SRE. The rewards of these systems include more durable and available storage.

The Role of Cardinality

*Charity Majors and
Liz Fong-Jones*

Honeycomb.io

In the context of databases, cardinality refers to the uniqueness of data values contained in a set. Low cardinality means that a column has a lot of duplicate values in its set. High cardinality means that the column contains a large percentage of completely unique values. A column containing a single value will always be the lowest possible cardinality. A column containing unique IDs will always be the highest possible cardinality.

For example, if you had a collection of a hundred million user records, you can assume that userID numbers will have the highest possible cardinality. First name and last name will be high cardinality, though lower than userID because some names repeat. A field like gender would be fairly low cardinality, given the nonbinary but finite choices it could have. A field like species would be the lowest possible cardinality, presuming all of your users are humans.

Cardinality matters for observability, because high-cardinality information is the most useful data for debugging or understanding a system. Consider the usefulness of sorting by fields like user IDs, shopping cart IDs, request IDs, or myriad other IDs such as instances, container, build number, spans, and so forth. Being able to query against unique IDs is the best way to pinpoint individual needles in any given haystack.

Unfortunately, metrics-based tooling systems can only deal with low-cardinality dimensions at any reasonable scale. Even if you only have merely hundreds of hosts to compare, with metrics-based systems, you can't use hostname as an identifying tag without hitting the limits of your cardinality key space. These inherent limitations place unintended restrictions on the ways that data can be interrogated. When debugging with metrics, for every question you may want to ask of your data, you have to decide—in advance, before a bug occurs—what you need to inquire about so that its value can be recorded when that metric is written.

That inherent limitation has two big implications. First, if during the course of investigation you decide that an additional question must be asked to discover the source of a potential problem, that cannot be done after the fact. You must first set up the metrics that might answer that question and wait for the problem to happen again. Second, because it requires another set of metrics to answer that additional question, most metrics-based tooling vendors will charge you for recording that data. Your cost increases linearly with every new way you decide to interrogate your data to find hidden issues you could not have possibly predicted in advance.

Conversely, observability tools encourage developers to gather rich telemetry for every possible event that could occur, passing along the full context of any given request and storing it for possible use at some point down the line. Observability tools are specifically designed to query against high cardinality data. What that means for debugging is that you can interrogate your event data in any number of arbitrary ways. You can ask new questions that you did not need to predict in advance and find answers to those questions, or clues that will lead you to ask the next question. You repeat that pattern again and again, until you find the needle that you're looking for in the proverbial haystack.

Adapted from the upcoming book *Observability Engineering*, expected in 2021 from O'Reilly.

Security Is like an Onion

Lucas Fontes

Auth0

Your company is living the dream. You've found product–market fit, sales are growing, and the idea of an IPO or acquisition steadily inches closer to reality. One day, the leadership team brings in external help to navigate the IPO process, and the conversation goes like this:

> *Consultant*: Everything is looking great! So tell us, how's your security story?

> *Leadership*: Well, we haven't been hacked so I would say it is pretty good!

> *Consultant*: How do you know you haven't been hacked? What is your exposure?

> *Leadership*: (stares into the abyss) I will get back to you on that.

As an SRE, one of your goals is to guide security controls and confidently answer questions related to risk management; but where should you start? I like the NIST's CyberSecurity framework of Identify, Protect, Detect, Respond, and Recover. Use it as is or as a foundation for your own security journey.

Identify what is crucial to business continuity in terms of systems, data, and assets. Once identified, evaluate the risk associated with each concern and any changes required to achieve the desired state by asking questions such as: What is preventing someone from interacting with our servers at our colocation data center? How do we deal with misplaced laptops or phones?

To get started here, you'll want to familiarize yourself with device encryption and basic mobile device management (MDM), because it can improve your security without jeopardizing usability.

Unpleasant cybersecurity events are a fact of life. The *protect* function is about limiting or containing the impact when one occurs. The keys are training, continuity, and supply chain management. Ensure that everyone goes through training related to identity management, privileged data manipulation, and remote access. Document and exercise controls for business continuity and disaster recovery. Finally, implement protective measures for the code supply chain, such as code scanning and use of third-party licenses.

A good *detection* system should have layers, raising an alarm each time one layer fails. The most important property of a detection system is its mean time to detection, which dictates how quickly you can react to a cybersecurity incident. The goal is for anomalies and events to be detected and their potential impact understood. Again, make sure to exercise the detection system manually, validating its accuracy.

"Plans are useless, but planning is indispensable." How will you *respond*? Plan activities related to an imminent or ongoing cybersecurity incident. How will you determine the blast radius of the attack? What about isolating the attack's damage? One often forgotten part is identifying internal and external communication channels that need to be notified about the incident. Remember to consider whether the channels can be compromised as part of the attack.

Last, *recover*. Life always moves forward. That means we need to think of how we come back from cybersecurity incidents. This should include a reflection on the incident and guide changes to the framework to prevent similar incidents and increase organizational and customers' confidence. Externally, this means a write-up in the form of an incident review for regaining public trust. Internally, you must review changes made during the incident and their impact on current playbooks, monitoring, and detection systems.

Security is a journey and will never be complete. By embracing a security framework, your team will be able to identify and respond to incidents in a timely fashion. Constantly learn from previous incidents and reassess your baseline. The world of cybersecurity is vast and, hopefully, this helped guide you in this journey!

Use Your Words

Tanya Reilly

Squarespace

When it comes to reliability, we're used to discussing new advances in the field, but one of the most powerful forces for reliability is also one of the oldest: the ancient art of writing things down. A culture of documenting our ideas helps us design, build, and maintain reliable systems. It lets us uncover misunderstandings before they lead to mistakes, and it can take critical minutes off outage resolution.

Code is a precise form of communication. A pull-request reviewer can mentally step through a change and evaluate exactly what it does. What they can't say, though, is whether it *should* do that thing. That's why thorough *PR descriptions* are so important. To evaluate whether a change is really safe, a reviewer needs to understand what the code author is trying to achieve. Our words need to be precise too.

Words give us a shared reality. They force us to be honest with ourselves. A system design that felt quite reasonable during whiteboard discussions might have glaring holes once the author is confronted with describing an actual migration or deployment plan or admitting their security strategy is "hope nobody notices us." An *RFC* or *design document* spells out our assumptions. They let us read each other's minds.

A culture of writing things down reduces ambiguity and helps us make better decisions. For example, an availability SLO of 99.9% only tells you anything if you know what the service's owners consider "available" to mean. If there's an accompanying *SLO definition document* that explains that a one-second response is considered a success, and you were hoping for 10-millisecond latencies, you'll reevaluate whether this back end is the one for you.

Once decisions are made, *lightweight architectural decision records* leave a trail to explain the context in which the decision was made, what trade-offs the team considered, and why they chose the path they did. Without these records, future maintainers of systems may be confronted with a Chesterton's gate: a mysterious component that seems unnecessary but that could be critical to reliability.

Writing shortens incidents too. During an outage, written *playbooks*—documentation optimized for reading by a stressed-out person who was just paged—can remind an on-caller how a system works, where its code lives, what it depends on, and who should be contacted, saving brain cycles and valuable minutes for debugging.

For long incidents, *incident-state documents* can record who's involved, which avenues are being explored, and which temporary fixes will need to be cleaned up, making it much easier to hand over when an on-caller or incident commander needs a break. If that information is only stored in one person's head, they'll want to push through tiredness and stay involved in the incident, even if their senses are dulled and their decisions are no longer the safest ones. After the incident, *written retrospectives* help us learn from our own mistakes and from each other.

Writing takes longer in the short term. It's definitely easier to start coding without a written design, to assure yourself that you'll remember the takeaways from an incident, to assume that everyone just understands each other. But if you take a little extra time to describe what's happening, using words, you'll help other people save time by reading your mind. Even your own future self may be grateful for the notes you write now.

You can't do SRE well without investing in a culture of communication. Writing is good for reliability, the more precise the better. Take time to get good at it.

Where to SRE

Fatema Boxwala

Facebook

SREs are a very hot commodity right now; companies need a lot of them, and there are not that many out there. The first thing to know when choosing a job: you are valuable. It can give you the confidence that the first offer you get probably isn't the only one you'll have.

However, the first offer you get might be uniquely valuable to *you*. The decision about where to work should be 100% informed by what *you* need and value right now. You might need to take the first position you're offered - for any number of reasons. I've been in that place myself, and that's perfectly fine.

When you have the opportunity to decide between positions, it can be hard to figure out what to do! This is especially true if you are new to the field or entering from a nontraditional path. To decide, you must know what you value most in a job and what you can expect from companies.

Does it matter to you what kind of people you work with? Do you prefer to be on a team that is more social and outgoing, or would you rather keep your work and social lives separate? Both are totally fine ways to be; you just have to determine which one you like best.

How much money do I need, and how soon do I need it? Although it's easy to calculate which offer is the most valuable, you might have different priorities. Big cash sign-on bonuses might not be as valuable as stock units that gain value over time, but you might find a big influx of cash critical right now. Think about money in terms of your actual needs and not in terms of the technically most optimal answer.

Sometimes benefits are lumped in with money. They're part of your compensation, so it might make sense to think about them in a strictly monetary fashion. However, it's best to think about benefits separately. For example, some health plans might be more monetarily valuable than others, but they might not include something important to your life, like birth control.

If you are working in a country where you are not a citizen, some companies will be able to offer you better job and immigration security than others. Larger companies with offices all over the world often have contingency plans for employees if something goes wrong with their immigration, whereas smaller startups do not have those resources.

You might care a lot about working somewhere that has a mission and purpose that align with your moral values. Not working for a company because it has practices that you morally disagree with—and making it clear that this is the reason you're not working there—can be a powerful act.

Thinking critically about how your work will impact the world is a critical factor when choosing a job. However, just like having any options at all, it's also a privilege. It might not be one that you have right now, especially if you are new to the field or disadvantaged in other ways.

As SREs, we often have the privilege of options. When you spend most of your waking hours at your job, you owe it to yourself to be informed about what your options are, and how you can make the most of them. Hopefully, this guide has helped you start to think about that!

Dear Future Team

Frances Rees

Google

Don't get too excited, I'm not looking to move yet, but it's fun to imagine what team #4 will be like. There are, of course, the important questions: What do you work on? How big is the team? Who are the other teams you work with? And then there are the questions that go beyond the formal interviews and role descriptions.

Here's what I hope is true.

I hope you eat lunch together. Maybe not every day, but I hope you can talk to each other outside of meetings. I hope you can introduce me to all the teams nearby and point out the one to ask about this tool, that kind of bug, or the other shared service.

I hope you ask lots of questions. Questions you feel a little awkward about asking because you think they might be dumb or obvious. Questions about how things work, why things are the way they are, why you do things the way you do, what value you're trying to add with a project. Questions you're not even sure have an answer.

I hope you love telling stories as much as I do. Stories of achievements, hard-learned lessons, or just funny things you've discovered. I believe that it's important to remember and preserve the tales of the team, to feel connected to what happened before you joined the team and feel that you can build on it.

My first team prided ourselves on drawing a map of Maps for anyone who would listen, with every funny story of how we ended up with dependency cycles, components with the same name besides an underscore, and how it's tedious to expand the name of TDS. The best kind of decorations are whiteboards that spawn architecture diagrams like weeds that grow richer over time and draw a crowd of interested onlookers to ask questions.

I hope this makes you the loudest team on the floor, debating new ideas with vigor, listening to everyone, and disagreeing technically without fighting personally. I hope you have big ideas and aren't afraid to try them. That you believe the way things have been until now doesn't have to stay forever. I hope people are excited about what they're working on and feel proud of the impact it will have.

I hope you trust that your manager has your back. I hope that they support you if things don't go to plan, celebrate if you succeed, suggest ideas if you're stuck, find opportunities if you're bored, and gather help if you're overloaded. I hope that if what you really need them to do is simply listen, without judgment and without offering solutions, that they will.

I hope you're truly partners with your developers. For a long time, I spent half my days sitting with one of my developer teams, the web services, and they quickly stopped worrying that something was broken when I walked up. I bought a token for their weekly build cop—the day before we found out their project was moved to another country. Sid the stuffed spider still sits on my desk to remind me how much we built together.

I hope you have fun with each other as a team and feel comfortable being yourselves together. After all, that's what teams are for.

And I hope you like puns.

Regards,

Your future teammate

Sustainability and Burnout

Denise Yu

GitHub

Building, running, and being part of an SRE team is a marathon, not a sprint. Incident response in many organizations is an inherently high-stress situation, and repeated out-of-hours escalations can easily contribute to cycles of professional burnout. As we fine-tune SLOs and iterate on rotation design, it's equally important to keep touch on the pulse of the health of the team, and constantly ask: As a group, are we working in a way that is sustainable over the long haul?

What does burnout look like? Burnout is, fortunately, a well-studied clinical condition; doctors like Dr. Herbert Freudenberger, starting in the 1970s, have researched and characterized burnout as having three telltale signs:

- Emotional exhaustion: too much time spent on caring too much
- Depersonalization: you find yourself empathizing less with others
- Decreased sense of accomplishment

The signs of burnout will of course manifest differently in every individual and, if you're an individual like me, who places a lot of pressure on themselves, learning to recognize our own emotional states is not a muscle we've spent much time developing, which makes having high-trust conversations about our well-being all the more difficult.

A group of technologists and researchers created an online questionnaire (*https://burnoutindex.org*) that your team can take to assess risk levels for burnout specifically within the tech industry.

I learned from a talk by Drs. Emily and Amelia Nagoski that burnout is, in part, caused by unresolved *feedback loops*. That deeply resonated with me; I have worked on many teams where experiments were never concluded, because we failed to close the needed feedback loops deliberately, which led to a state of uncertainty and anxiety about whether we were becoming more effective.

It would be unacceptable to launch a feature without measurable success criteria in most healthy product organizations. Similarly, healthy teams should regularly introspect on *how* they're working. The most common tool is to have regular retrospectives (I'd recommend beginning with a weekly cadence, then iterating), but many teams also use health checks, such as the model created by Spotify. Measuring team health will be largely qualitative, but that doesn't make it any less important than, say, uptime numbers; you can only troubleshoot a team that's burning out if you can catch early warning signs.

I'll close out by briefly touching on psychological safety and its role in creating sustainable teams. Extensive research has been performed over the years to show that psychological safety is a nonnegotiable cornerstone for building learning organizations. Psychological safety is the set of "perceptions of the consequences of taking interpersonal risks in a particular context such as a workplace."

With greater safety, people are more inclined to provide dissenting feedback to their teams and try innovative experiments that carry greater risk than continuing with business as usual. These are important avenues for course correction, and they're inaccessible to teams that have a pattern of punishing anyone who disagrees with the majority or with individuals in positions of power.

There is no dark art to building sustainable, healthy teams. Teams are unique organisms; every team will have a slightly different group dynamic, with different responses to the same stimuli, but there are common traits. Sustainable teams have the capacity to learn and improve continuously, which is critical for building effective SRE organizations. Safe teams have access to a richer set of indicators for success or failure. These indicators contribute directly to a team's ability to close those feedback loops, which in turn, enable teams to feel productive and healthy.

Don't Take Advice from Graybeards

John Looney

Facebook

Don't take advice from graybeards just because they seem confident. No one has any idea where the tech industry is going. Hedge your bets; 90% of predictions turn out hilariously wrong. The first career advice I got was, "With MS-DOS 6.1, the world doesn't need any more software. Go into hardware." The second was, "No one pays for generalists; you need to specialize." Now I'm an SRE.

Heinlein told me, "Specialization is for insects." Try a stint as a software engineer. Sysadmin. Front end. Back end. Hardware. Product. Bartender. Founder. Learn something new every birthday.

Burnout is a bitch. It will happen a few times, and each time you think, "I'll never fall for that again." Again, you will work too hard, too long, without reward or appreciation. It can permanently damage your health. The young and invincible assume it won't happen to them. Life is a marathon, not a sprint.

Maybe you'll be a manager; maybe you won't. You could work for a famous multinational or always be in startups no one heard of. Your stock options might be worth millions. You might build something that makes you famous in the eyes of people you respect. *Blindboy* warned me not to put my "locus of evaluation" into other people's hands—even my mother's. And he wears a plastic bag on his head.

Mental health isn't binary. Plomin taught me there are thousands of genetic mutations that make small differences in what we are good at, how much stamina we have, and how we are motivated. We need to keep experimenting to find out what works for us and the ones we care about. Find someone you respect in every company you work in and ask them to be your mentor. Listen to their advice, even if you don't take it.

The more money you have, the more you need. You can read a book under a nearby tree for $5 and it'll give you as much pleasure as reading it on a beach halfway around the planet. You can move to The Valley, do 60-hour weeks, make senior and 500k a year in five years, but you won't realize the friends, your health, and self-respect you've lost.

Ensure that you have walkout money so that you can leave bad employers. Feeling financially trapped makes situations far worse. Dilemmas get easier when you ask, "In ten years, what will I wish I'd done?" Your current salary and job dictate the next one. In a boom time, employers have to hire people who can't do the job yet, but they almost always meet the challenge. Make sure you are only 80% sure you can do the jobs you apply for, or you aren't stretching yourself. Women should probably apply when they are only 60% sure, because they've been conditioned not to believe how tremendously competent they are.

We work for managers, not companies. Managers aren't your friends, they are your agents. Fire them if you don't like the community, work, or money they bring you. Marie Kondo told me there are only two reasons for not letting go: an attachment to the past or a fear of the future. She's likely never needed a VGA cable in an emergency, though.

Don't build a framework when a shell script will do. Don't write a shell script if it's likely to be in revision control for more than a few weeks. Fred Brooks told me not to hire coders until I've designed the system, but what would he know? He also recommended two secretaries per programming team.

Don't take advice from graybeards just because they sound confident.

Facing That First Page

Andrew Louis

DigitalOcean

In 2017, straight out of college, I started to learn the ropes at a software engineering gig at Shopify. During the year-long run-up to my first on-call shift, I spent hours reading the #war-room Slack channel, captivated by the fluency of that day's responding engineers as they corralled a terrifying page into a coordinated, calm, and focused incident response, cutting across multiple teams.

That first page is no joke. I hope to make it easier for you with some light structure and tools to help navigate the uncertainty of being paged your first time.

Consider your emotional response. It felt like the senior engineers had ice running through their veins, but the truth of the matter is that *everyone* gets a little bit anxious.

If you find yourself there, it's okay to take a quick moment, take stock of your nerves, gather yourself, and move forward. Reach out to a colleague if you're overwhelmed or find yourself ill-equipped for a particular incident response; it's okay to feel this way, but it *is important* to ask for the help you need in the interest of navigating to a faster resolution.

Then ask, *"What's hurting right now?"* You probably got an alert that described a dramatic change in some key business metric. You could embark on several paths with this page, so first, very simply: try to localize *what is affected*, not to assess scale or blast radius but, instead, just with your best effort of mapping the alert to the systems affected. What could make this challenging is the disconnect between the alerting metric and the systems themselves that are affected.

Your organizational knowledge of key metrics and the systems behind them could be leveraged here to support this investigation, which you will build up as time goes on, but in its absence, you can try to understand what the cross-organizational alerting *correlations* are.

Here, you can leverage your tooling. For example, getting a high-level view of the other ongoing pages or alerts being triggered (through Slack searches, PagerDuty, Bugsnag, etc.) can help you do a reasonable job of identifying the impacted systems.

Next, *whom do you page?* After identifying the systems affected, you *may* have to figure out whom to page. Although it's your pager that's sounding off, perhaps you've narrowed an upstream dependency to be a likely culprit.

Sometimes it's you, but what if it's not? It's easy to find someone to page; the hard part is the doubt. What if it's the wrong page? You could be waking up an engineer in mid-REM sleep, only to have them tell you that you dialed the wrong number.

You *might* make the wrong page sometimes. At this point, however, trust the facts that you've accumulated thus far and continue to act quickly. Chances are, even if the page was incorrect, your due diligence would seem to indicate that the degrees of separation between the wrong recipient and the right one are limited.

Above all, remember to savor the moment. Your first page will be terrifying, but the magic feeling of the transformation—watching a faint alert build up to a large-scale incident response—will feel like an absolute nerd flex. Everyone starts somewhere, and although you might put pressure on yourself to ace it the first, second, or third time, remember that you're just building the neural pathways you need to gain the fluency we all aspire to.

PART II

Zero to One

SRE, at Any Size, Is Cultural

Matthew Huxtable

Ziglu

Today's modern business environments are complex places that move fast with limited resources in pursuit of continually delivering customer value. Maintaining reliable systems is an intricate, detail-oriented task that is difficult to prioritize in this broader context. Traditionally, the effort required to build systems while maintaining production uptime has been little understood, an implicit requirement in the margins, the burden delegated to technical teams.

Leaders make this trade-off at their peril. An understanding of expected reliability and a well-developed risk thermostat are not cutesy optional extras; today, they are first-class requirements. Although engineers and leaders understand this, hierarchies and lack of shared context across an organization are a hazard that prevents development of an integrated approach to building reliable systems.

SRE ushers cultures that recognize these challenges. Through quantitative means, SRE makes explicit the relationship between operational reliability and customer happiness. By prioritizing long-term, objective measures of success, SRE facilitates continual negotiations of reliability whose outcomes are supported by broader organizational objectives. Done well, it emphasizes the importance of humans in continually creating the conditions for success, rather than emphasizing each omission that leads to failure.

For example, although many aspects of SRE adoption are an implementation detail for each organization, *error budgets* are considered a basic, immutable property by which the efficacy of any SRE culture may be judged. Distilling reliability into a single, easily comprehensible number and radiating this throughout the organization promotes a shared language of reliability as a first-class concern. Treating reliability as just another business metric enables it to be negotiated and traded where other business requirements take precedence.

However, despite SRE's deep roots in quantitative analysis, it is ironic that successful adoption and maintenance of SRE culture remains coupled to the soft skills of its practitioners. Personal relationships, shared trust, and eschewing power relationships arising from hierarchy are essential for a successful SRE culture to emerge. Such cultural adoption provides an opportunity to level the playing field and work together to achieve success—but embracing these opportunities is key.

We often hear the refrain that faithful adoption of SRE cannot be achieved by rebadging an existing infrastructure or operations teams. The efforts and personal sacrifices of engineers are meaningless if they do not resonate at a strategic level. Likewise, calculated risks leaders take cannot be understood or quantified without shared language by which to communicate them. It is for these reasons that a traditional ops team cannot become SRE overnight. The Space Shuttle *Challenger* was approved for launch by NASA managers seeking to avoid delays in an already beleaguered schedule, despite known engineer concerns about the safety of the orbiter vehicle in subzero launch temperatures. When engineers engineer and leaders lead in isolated vacuums, introspective behaviors, shared empathy, and mutual trust for each other cannot flourish.

SRE offers a shared language for leveling the playing field between engineers and leaders—the quantitative means of prioritizing and integrating the conflicting goals of keeping the lights on with the need to remain competitive through delivering new functional value to stakeholders and customers. However, practicing SRE sustainably is fundamentally an organizational problem, one of effective communication, trust, and autonomy, all of which are hard to acquire and easy to lose, especially when team bandwidth to focus on its adoption is limited.

Successful SRE adoption is about so much more than automating your software operations. It's cultural.

Everyone Is an SRE in a Small Organization

Matthew Huxtable

Ziglu

"Site reliability engineering is the answer."

Or so I thought, when I talked myself into my first SRE role in a small software company a few years ago. At last, a mechanism existed that articulated my work as a software engineer and systems operator—the ultimate exception handler of last resort when things go awry. The opportunity to adopt and implement the same approach for operations as is used by large multinational organizations ought to be exciting to anyone. However, it became clear that success would require going off script.

The SRE approach in small organizations is challenging. Resources are constrained, talent acquisition is hard, and the customer base cannot be taken for granted. The SRE practitioner's task overwhelmingly combines a multitude of roles in seeking to do more with less. A technical background in engineering, systems administration, or operations is unlikely to be sufficient. Success in SRE requires deep emotional understanding, influence, and organizational context to advocate for change and foster a blameless engineering culture. Success in SRE means building a culture that prioritizes user happiness, an outcome only attainable when operating at the intersection of technical know-how and human factors.

Contrary to the standard textbook approach, creating a dedicated SRE resource in these smaller organizations is best achieved by sharing responsibility broadly. It is challenging for new SRE teams to carve out their own niche and empower others when success is measured in terms of delivering features to customers. Reliability is unlikely to be a first-class strategic concern; it cannot be assumed to be axiomatic and might only arise infrequently as a matter of inconvenience when blindsided by an unexpected outage.

When each new feature drives measurable growth and increases the utility of the service, everyone has an incentive to deliver whatever value is necessary to preserve their future livelihoods, and that's likely to mean new features.

Calibration of the organizational risk thermostat is more ad hoc and imprecise, driven by emotional motivations rather than quantitative judgments. You may not even need a dedicated focus on reliability; early adopters of a service will often tolerate relatively poor uptime!

Embracing the idea "you build it, you run it" empowers everyone in your organization with shared responsibility for reliability and makes broad use of your team's skills. In addition, through sharing the pain of running production services, opportunities to develop shared empathy and technical understanding which will be necessary at scale are improved.

Similarly, practitioners implementing SRE must be careful to favor ideas that promote shared context over centralized control. This example commonly arises in misguided attempts to aid quality management, such as handing back a pager in response to perceived excesses in operational toil. Unfortunately, reprioritizing a priority queue of size one yields no appreciable change in its order. For SRE at small scale, there is only one production service to support, and there are significant personal and organizational incentives to continue to offer that support. Favoring shared responsibility and conversation over additional friction is more likely to be fruitful in the long run.

Software systems continue to increase in complexity. With broad and evolving community support, SRE offers a model for sustainably growing such systems that is sufficiently flexible for organizations of all sizes. The most successful implementations understand the importance of sharing responsibility and reducing friction, all in the pursuit of customer success.

Auditing Your Environment for Improvements

Joan O'Callaghan

Udemy

Adopting a SRE (site reliability engineering) mindset doesn't only start after your first official SRE project. What can you do with no SRE staff when you want to make your company more reliable? The first step is to review what you already have. You need to know your environment better. Audit it and record the risks. Start with your worst-case scenario. Security breaches, data loss, and downtime are bad for everyone, but what would destroy *your* business? Know your kryptonite and focus on that first.

Next, move on to capacity. If you don't know your limits, you can't keep safe or plan your growth. Determine whether you have any capacity issues. How much headroom do you have, if any? What is the lead time to get more of anything? Dig into whether you have peak traffic or usage patterns.

Another important area is security. At a fast-moving organization, unfortunately, this can be overlooked until it becomes a problem. Who has access to what, and when people leave, are they properly off-boarded? Do you have a password manager, and have you turned on audit logs for your cloud accounts? How many people can destroy your company?

With infrastructure needs, you want to think about backups. Start by making a fast infrastructure diagram—just whiteboard it and take a photo. Is there one of anything? Is it all reproducible? Practice reproducing parts of it during nonemergency times, document the process, and always remember to test your backups.

Next, consider third parties that your business relies on, such as hosting providers, DNS, and security. Go through your billing/invoices to make sure you know about all the third parties you use for engineering-related services. Build a list and, in some cases, consider redundant/backup links. Do you have details (such as support number and account number) for each of them on a wiki? Update the contact details with these companies to ensure that they email to a list of people rather than just to one person in your company.

Another area that is very easy to forget about is domains and SSL certs. That can cause a huge amount of damage to your business if neglected. Do you know all the domains critical to your business? Do you have logons to all the domain registrars you use? How do you notify about expirations? Even setting up a calendar reminder is better than nothing. Last, document your update procedures—it is possible to have five certs all with different update requirements, so make sure they are documented. If you have a renewal cadence of three years, chances are that some knowledge has been lost.

After you complete your review, choose some tasks. You want to make the maximum amount of improvement but in a limited amount of time. Timebox your efforts and start off with two hours a week to allow for small but steady progress. Make sure your boss is okay with your time being spent on this. Don't get overwhelmed by the massive amount of work to be done. Do not try to take on *another* full-time job. You risk burnout and reduce the likelihood that your company will provide you with more SRE resources. Why hire someone else if you are doing this work too?

You can't fix it all. It is just not possible, even with a full team of SREs! We're not aiming for perfection; we're just looking for *better*. You're adding SRE to your company one task at a time and making things better. Just keep going, and good luck! Don't stress. Things will always break; it is a normal part of engineering. This is not your main job, and even if you get the green light to reduce some of your other tasks, it is just not possible to fix it all, even with a full team of SRE engineers!

You are adding SRE to your company one task at a time and making things better. Just keep going, and good luck!

With Incident Response, Start Small

Thai Wood

Resilience Roundup

There's a good chance that your incident response plan looks something like the following:

1. Someone gets paged (possibly you!)
2. ???
3. Fix it

That's the plan that develops in many cases on its own. As your organization and systems grow—in the number of people that operate it, the number of people it serves, or its complexity—that plan no longer fits. As part of an SRE or Ops team, you can watch for some of these signs:

- You're unsure how to start an incident.
- You don't know how or when to get more people involved.
- You don't know whether to start a call or conference bridge or use chat.
- There's no consistent way to notify people who might be affected by the incident.
- When battling the incident, it's unclear who is doing what.

An *incident* by its very nature is a surprising event, a cognitively difficult task. Not being able to answer these questions introduces further uncertainty to an incident and can be incredibly costly. Instead of trying to investigate and solve the mystery of the incident directly, responders are trying to answer those questions by figuring out how to coordinate from scratch instead of attacking the problem. The results are split focus by the responders and longer downtimes.

Taking steps to change this pattern can be difficult. It can feel impossible to find the time or space to learn or make a new plan, especially if many incidents have occurred lately. Fortunately, it's possible to start small. How do you move from flying by the seat of your pants to operating within a framework? Take small steps, with the understanding that when dealing with complex, unpredictable things, the plan can't specify everything. You will never know what kind of incident might occur, because you can't predict the future, so investing in an incident response framework helps shift focus away from many of the little decisions that need to be made in the moment toward the mystery of the incident itself.

After working with many teams in all sorts of organizations, I've found that a pretty good starting point is to think in terms of three roles: incident manager, expert/operator, and communications. If you're the one who is paged, you're wearing all those hats at the moment you answer. Anytime you don't have someone to fill that role, you fill it. Except for incident manager, you can have any number of the other roles that makes sense; usually, this only applies to the expert/operator role, but some folks like to split internal and external communications.

Once you have someone else in the expert/operator role, your focus should shift primarily to keeping track of what is going on. Know that that is a lot to ask of one person, especially if they're still taking on multiple roles. You'll be focusing on things such as who is doing what, whether the response seems stuck, and who might need replacing due to fatigue.

I'll admit that working this way takes practice. I recommend that teams practice together without much technology involved, such as by using some tabletop exercises. It's also something you can practice mentally as you are on call. Continue to ask yourself, "What role am I operating in now?"

The most important part about an incident response framework is that it exists. It needs to exist out of one person's head. It needs to exist in a form that can be seen by others and practiced. Soon enough, small steps will lead to big results.

Solo SRE: Effecting Large-Scale Change as a Single Individual

Ashley Poole

Boomin

Being a solo SRE in an organization typically comes about through one of two paths: you already have past SRE experience and you're joining the organization as its first SRE hire, or you're an engineer within your existing organization and you've seen how introducing an SRE culture and practice could improve pain points and ultimately improve your product life cycle.

As a solo SRE, it might seem daunting at first to see a possibly endless list of pain points that need solving. Often this includes recurring production outages, possibly even from a handful of common root causes. Can you really effect that change on the scale needed? Yes!

When deciding what to tackle first, review the most common or most impactful pain points and find a small area where you can make the most impact, given your likely limited available time between fighting fires. Often, some of the biggest wins include lack of observability, unstructured incident management, or inadequate testing and release procedures.

Without observability, how do you determine how your product (that is, service) is performing, its health, or your users' happiness?! Improving observability could be anything from implementing logging, adding appropriate logging context, adding or configuring monitoring, exposing metrics, or adding request tracing so that you can help debug failures when things go wrong because, let's face it, they will.

Incident management is a natural progress after observability, because you must first be able to detect an incident before you can manage it. Incident management focuses on how the incident is managed in a well-defined, clear, and structured process and supports documentation such as in runbooks, which provide detailed instructions on how to service a failure service.

Your incident management process should set out expectations and roles for managing an incident as well as the responsibilities of those roles. Typically, incident management roles include an incident commander, technical lead, and communications lead, although the size of the incident and the organization compliance requirements will often determine whether a single person handles all roles during an incident or different people handle them.

Inadequate testing and release procedures can often both be a source of incidents and prolong them unnecessarily when they occur. This is commonly caused by the lack of repeatability in procedures that typically involve heavily manual processes that can be error prone and slow to complete. Seeking opportunities that could benefit from automation is a great way to improve repeatability and reduce your cycle time for those operations.

By starting out small and getting some quick wins under your belt, you'll be able to demonstrate the positive benefits of SRE through incremental change and reduce daily toil for yourself or other engineers.

Demonstrating this positive change and involving others in the process is an important step to growing your SRE culture, and you'll soon notice that an increasing number of engineers will show a willingness to learn and embrace the SRE culture you're trying to build.

The most important point to remember in being a solo SRE is that although you can effect change within your organization, you cannot do it alone, so don't try to carry the weight of your organization's problems only on your own shoulders. The worst thing you could do for yourself and the organization is to try to take all that on yourself. In some extreme circumstances, this could lead to burnout. Your mental health is important. Remember that!

Design Goals for SLO Measurement

Ben Sigelman

LightStep

When designing for SLO measurement, consider the goals of flexibility, testability, freshness, cost, reliability, and organizational constraints. Let me explain how to use them. You want flexible targets. That is, SLOs must be able to evolve over time. Sometimes this is simply to adjust an error budget to allow for more releases and faster product iteration.

Operators should be able to adjust the heuristics embedded in the SLIs, (for example, 25 ms [milliseconds] to 30 ms), success thresholds (95% of the time to 97% of the time), aggregation windows (over the past 30 seconds to over the past 7 days), and more, all without making code changes, redeploying software, or pushing new production configuration. The SLO performance history before and after the target revision should also be retained, with some way to see how each target has changed over time.

Next, consider testable targets. When adding a new SLO, we need both an SLI and an objective, or target. Crafting appropriate targets is often subtle and challenging. What's the right error budget, given our reliability history? Percentile of latency to measure? Actual latency threshold? And, given our goal of *flexible* SLO targets, any time an SLO needs updating, these should all be reconsidered. To feel confident about our SLOs, backtest possible targets against historical data, especially when SLOs are involved in alerting—and estimate alert frequency when setting a threshold.

Freshness is a measure of the time it takes for an SLO to reflect real-time data in production. Lower time deltas are better as far as freshness is concerned, but the actual freshness requirements depend on the particular SLO.

Certain SLOs might only be used for monthly managerial reports, where it's immaterial whether the SLO incorporates data from the most recent 30 seconds. In other situations, SLOs are the first line of defense for business-critical production firefighting; then, freshness should be measured in seconds and data processing delays kept to a minimum.

Cost must be a design consideration, too. Implementing flexible, testable, fresh SLOs is much easier with an infinite budget, but the data-engineering requirements for effective organization-wide SLOs can be significant, especially for high-throughput or widely distributed applications. It's neither necessary nor realistic to estimate costs to multiple decimal places, but it *should* be possible to get within a factor of 10 by thinking ahead along three axes: *time series data, structured logging data,* and *opportunity cost.*

Just as individual services have SLOs, the SLO infrastructure must have SLOs of its own! Implement SLOs on top of or within existing high-availability observability components. Sometimes, though, SLOs are implemented through rickety scripts or poorly monitored cron jobs, introducing risk and unreliability. If you need to build net-new infrastructure to implement certain high-priority SLOs, so be it—but plan ahead and allocate time to make that net-new infrastructure highly available. SLO infrastructure must be among the most reliable software your organization runs in production.

Finally, organizations often bring constraints beyond any technical or budgetary considerations. For instance, it's still common for organizations in certain highly regulated industries to require all operational data to stay on premises, in physical data centers, or within the organization's VPC (virtual private cloud). In other cases, an organization will fight data silos by requiring all durable time series data or all structured logging data to reside within a particular database or with a particular vendor.

The goals outlined here aren't exhaustive, but your SLO implementation will be all the better for having considered and accounted for them! Remember this is just a model; you must do what works best for you, your systems, and your users.

Adapted from the book *Implementing Service Level Objectives: A Practical Guide to SLIs, SLOs, and Error Budgets* (*https://oreil.ly/kAVJt*) (O'Reilly).

I Have an Error Budget— Now What?

Alex Hidalgo

Nobl9

SLIs, SLOs, and error budgets are the bedrock of site reliability engineering. Much has been written about what they are, but not much has been written about how to use them. The classic example of, "Ship features when you have an error budget; halt releases and focus on reliability when you don't," is a bit archaic and doesn't really expose all of the great decisions you can make with your data.

So if it's not just about shipping features or not, what can we use error budget data for?

Well, I would be remiss if I didn't mention that you can, in fact, use error budgets to determine when to release new features. Changes to code or configuration are the single most common vector of new problems, so sometimes it actually is completely reasonable to say, "Let's slow down a little bit and figure out how to make things more stable." But let's spend some time talking about what other decisions you can make, using error budget data.

A more reasonable use of error budget data is to determine the focus of your project work. SLO-based approaches to reliability are about providing you with better data to have better discussions and make better decisions. Having a hard mandate about when to ship code probably doesn't make much sense in many situations, but using this data to help you figure out what your team should be focused on does make a lot of sense! You don't have to halt your release pipeline to be able to say, "We've been unreliable more than we've aimed to be—maybe for this next sprint, half the team focuses on fixing that instead of on feature work."

You can also use your error budget status to figure out when to experiment. You learn about systems when changes are introduced, so introduce changes on purpose to see how your service reacts! This could be anything from chaos engineering to performing failover exercises or even something like experimenting with a new algorithm or garbage collection method. Use your error budgets to figure out the right times to perform these experiments; if you've been too unreliable recently, perhaps it makes sense to hold off, but if you have lots of error budget remaining, do what you want!

Something a little bit scarier is just purposely burning your excess budget. If other services rely on yours, you need to make sure you're not being more reliable than you advertise. Turn your service off on purpose so teams that depend on your service can learn about how their service performs when you're not being reliable.

Finally, you can also just do nothing at all! If you have tons of error budget remaining, maybe you just leave things that way because your team has other urgent priorities. If you've burned through your budget even several times over, it might be the case that you're waiting for a shipment of new hardware to help fix things or perhaps you experienced a black swan event and there isn't a reasonable pivot to reliability work to make.

The point is that error budgets are about providing you with better data to make better decisions. If you have a meaningful SLI and a reasonable SLO, your error budget data helps you think about how you've been performing to user expectations and requirements over time. Use this data in whatever way makes the most sense for you.

How to Change Things

Joan O'Callaghan

Udemy

As an SRE, you might be trying to push through an initiative that you know is for the good of the company but cannot get it done without buy-in or effort from other teams—and right now, you're not getting either.

"While in theory we support you, we don't have the bandwidth to facilitate. Maybe next quarter."

"That change is unnecessary, it's fine as it is."

How can you push this change through? First, this change must be worth it to you. Do not go to all this effort for something you are ambivalent about. It must also have big-picture improvements, and the timing must work.

If you can't convince your manager that this change is worth it, stop now and pick another battle. It won't happen soon. Back down with grace and revisit it in six months or whenever anything happens that decreases the resistance. Your manager is constantly assessing employee time versus task value, so respect their decision.

Next step: go up. You and your manager need to have a meeting with the level above your manager, such as with your director.

- Explain why you want to do this now.
- List the benefits, risks, and probabilities of the change.
- Be ready to discuss impacts.
- Be ready to compromise.
- Discuss why other teams will protest.
- List risks if we don't make this change.
- Have a testing and deployment plan.
- Have rollback steps.

If they agree with the sentiment that this is a good thing to do and it's worth doing, discuss organizational resistance. The resistance could come from the peers of this director or from the staff of their peers.

Go up or sideways? At this point, your director might share the plan with their peers. However, if your director thinks that resistance from some other directors might be very difficult to shift, you can go up again. The project may need an executive sponsor, such as the VP (vice president) or CTO (Chief Technology Officer) level.

Your manager or director argues the case. They don't sugarcoat the issues and discuss the plan to deal with them. An engineering executive is unlikely to sponsor a project that starts a turf war and negatively impacts intra-engineering relationships.

If the change is worth it, the timing is right, you've shown enough forward planning, and the moons are aligned, congratulations, you've obtained their sponsorship.

What now? You go back down a level again. Your director has a meeting with the other directors, where they share the plan and the top-level sponsor says, "Yup, this is gonna happen." The outcome of this meeting should mean that the other engineering directors are reassured that you and your team will do your utmost to make it as easy as possible but also understand that the change is inevitable, so they might as well just go with it.

Show empathy for the impacted teams from the very beginning. You have to make it as easy as possible for everyone to do this. Schedule meetings at times convenient for the relevant teams, and you can hear their fears and pain points. Respect their concerns and brainstorm ways to mitigate obstacles. Build a deployment plan that works with their schedule.

Think through how you'll communicate the change to the organization. Before the change happens, give a presentation to engineering because it will help alleviate concerns, aid maintaining project momentum, and reduce resistance to requests for help during the project.

Make this a project that lifts everyone up, and they might let you do something similar again!

Methodological Debugging

Avishai Ish-Shalom and
Nati Cohen

ScyllaDB
Here Technologies

SREs often debug in production—under stress and flooded with information. Debugging can seem like a mysterious, innate trait, but luckily this is untrue; rather, you can follow a structured methodological process to pinpoint the problem, avoiding mistakes and cognitive biases.

1. *Triage*: In dealing with an incident, we first must make some meta-decisions quickly: What's the business impact? Are we handling this incident now or can it be deferred? Do we have time to debug it or should we employ an emergency failover procedure? Many of the answers are unknown before you begin debugging. Triage is a short phase to answer these questions quickly, before launching into a possibly long debugging process. However, you can go back to it at any point: think of triage as a fail-fast step to return to any time you have more data.

2. *Operational definition*: To solve an issue we decide is worth pursuing, we need to define it precisely and measurably ("it's slow" doesn't cut it). An operational definition has two main parts: a method of measurement (i.e., From where? With which tools? When? In which environment?) and an expected result of that measurement (e.g., "p99 of transaction X is consistently over 500 ms since 1 hour ago, should be under 100 ms"). This allows us to collaborate and verify that we have indeed solved the issue we are handling.

3. *Making the mental model of the system explicit*: That we don't immediately know what broke down is a strong indication that our mental model of the system is incomplete, if not misleading. Our mission is to refine this model incrementally until it is close enough to reality to explain the problem. Write down the model as a diagram or text. (Use whatever is comfortable for you.) You may be tempted to skip this; don't! Writing forces you to articulate your model, which helps find gaps and,

more important, makes your assumptions clear so you can iterate on them.

4. *Iterating on the model*: Once we have an explicit model, we can improve it iteratively until the problem is found—not very different from the scientific method (*https://oreil.ly/jl_vM*): formulate a hypothesis, define what data is needed to corroborate or reject the hypothesis, collect this data, and evaluate it to decide whether the hypothesis should be rejected. Remember, our measurements could be wrong, we may be sidetracked by various cognitive biases, or we might simply be subject to the limits of reductionist thinking.

5. *Reconstructing and validating*: The reconstruction phase is basically the reverse of the analysis we do when we create a hypothesis about our model. Instead of breaking the system down to parts and subsystems, we reconstruct the system from our assumed parts, using the measurements we have, and ask whether the sum of the parts explains the system we are seeing—often it does not. We could be missing a part, or perhaps the faults we found in one of the parts are not relevant to this incident (things are always failing somewhere!). It could also be the *interaction* between parts that explains what we are experiencing and not any single part.

6. *Next steps*: The core idea for methodological debugging is to make our mental model (*https://oreil.ly/X430o*) explicit to become aware of deviations between our model and reality. With any methodology, mastering it requires practice and training, such as using game days to train and improve your mental model of the system. To learn more, check out our SREcon 2018 debugging workshop.

How Startups Can Build an SRE Mindset

Tamara Miner

Improbable Games

At startups, SRE is often an afterthought behind shiny new features.

This could be because product or market fit is higher priority, or service level objectives (SLOs) aren't clearly aligned with customers' needs. Yet ignoring SRE means missing part of the puzzle. SRE is about being customer-focused —really understanding the experience and pain of using your product in the same ways that your customers will. It can (and should) be a mindset that is present in everyone at your company.

So how can you do this? Implement a way to know and measure what your customers care about—not just features but how those features perform. Having a well-defined set of engineering principles and release gates helps standardize production readiness across the company in terms of product experience—just ensure that your engineering teams go beyond aspirational feelings. Such principles set service-level expectations across the organization for features and products at different stages of development.

Imagine if marketing and sales understood the impact of reliability and were empowered to set product roadmap expectations properly for customers! For example, if you are adding webhooks to your service, the initial release could be as beta. Release gates for beta features might be: support ten thousand customers, SLO metrics live on internal dashboards, and rate limits are set much lower than in production features. Without much interdepartmental communication overhead, the commercial teams already have what they need for customer communication.

The key to all this is bringing commercial teams along throughout the software development life cycle so that everyone has the right expectations and can be proactive about scale expectations, prioritization, and roadmap setting. Regardless of the stage of development, it is critical to understand the bottlenecks in your system and communicate them to stakeholders. Doing this properly should prevent your sales and marketing teams from over-promising to customers and facilitate continued communication between the engineers who know the systems, and the commercial teams who engage with customers should minimize the number of surprises when onboarding large new customers.

How do you make this happen? Make the process as self-serve as possible by internally publishing your value-based roadmap with a clear update cadence, so that any stakeholder can look up the next biggest challenge and raise red flags as needed. Increase engagement by having a sort of cross-departmental scrum-of-scrums to manage expectations, maximize the feeling of shared ownership (e.g., error budgets), and enable commercial teams to inform and advise on big, potential opportunities in the business's best interest.

There is likely to be a strong push to ignore SRE capability work and focus on new features, but this is when you point to those engineering and product principles and release gates to say, "Customers can live without a feature they haven't bought, even if they want it. They can't live without something that they bought and expected to work. Go down that path and they're likely to churn." Watch out for organizational assumptions about product reliability, scalability, and observability. To mitigate, use Kano models to demonstrate trade-offs in customer satisfaction between features and SRE concepts. (Note: demand forecasting can also be a powerful tool to help the business scale appropriately.)

To build a customer-focused product experience, bring business stakeholders to consensus on value-based outcomes (e.g., happy customers who promote your super-reliable brand). Help them understand how production readiness affects brand reputation and requires participation from all corners of the business. Don't fight the product; bring it along in the journey to establish an SRE mindset.

Bootstrapping SRE in Enterprises

Vanessa Yiu

Before embarking on bootstrapping SRE in large enterprises, it is essential to understand the key problems your organization needs to solve, and identify areas where SRE will have the most impact. These should be the primary drivers for your business case, and key deliverables on your roadmap. Broadly speaking, larger organizations tend to suffer more from runtime inefficiencies due to scale. Investing in SRE reduces operational overhead (and hence budget) on running production, and a common incentive is increasing developer productivity and cycles spent on driving strategic change.

However, how this problem manifests itself is much more nuanced. For example, services with higher service level maturity likely have well-established operational practices in place already but perhaps more instability due to usage growth (i.e., capacity constraints) and increasing complexity over time compared to newer services. Know that there is no one size fits all when it comes to implementation. Take the time to do research; interview product managers and on-call engineers to understand common challenges and leverage data sets (e.g., problem management database, incident post-mortems) where available to confirm trends and remove recency bias.

Once you can articulate a clear business case for SRE, securing sponsorship at the executive level sets the right level of focus for implementation. Stakeholder buy-in from other tech leads and managers is crucial to build partnership and scale across the organization. Standalone systems are rare in enterprises—the service you operate will probably depend on a range of other upstream and downstream services, so your success is directly correlated with your ability to navigate, influence, and deliver across the organization. Define clear roles and responsibilities for your stakeholders, as well as what they can expect from SRE for every engagement. To manage expectations, agree on a common set of measurable goals and deliverables each quarter. Check in regularly on progress, more frequently (e.g., weekly) at the start of any engagement until things reach steady state.

Textbook implementations of SRE rarely translate well in enterprises, given the diversity of businesses, products, and services and the complexity of organizational structures, environments, and systems that have grown organically over time. However, for most enterprises, introducing SLOs and error budgets to business-critical services remains a key differentiator for establishing SRE, so likely a core part of any implementation roadmap. If SLOs are not a status quo in your organization, be prepared to invest a significant amount of time in teaching stakeholders about the importance of SLOs and how to instrument meaningful ones as a step toward establishing this as common language across the organization.

At the outset, focus on solving a few key issues where SRE can demonstrate the most impact in the short term. These early successes build trust with the stakeholders mentioned earlier, demonstrate how SRE adds value to those unfamiliar with the discipline, help secure sustained investment, and ultimately increase your likelihood of success in the long run. Build on this incrementally by driving strategic change programs in parallel.

Be thoughtful about how to measure return on investment over time—progress, results, and success criteria for any engagement should always be quantifiable. These can take many forms, from SLO improvements, toil work measurement reduction, and achieving OKRs (objectives and key results), through to client satisfaction surveys. In addition, solicit open and honest feedback from stakeholders regularly. These are all powerful mechanisms to refine your approach and iterate plans based on what is working well or not for the organization.

Building a successful team in any large enterprise is no easy feat—and even more so for disciplines like SRE, where success depends on major cultural changes across the organization in addition to technical delivery. But it is possible!

It's Okay Not to Know, and It's Okay to Be Wrong

Todd Palino

LinkedIn

At LinkedIn, one of our core values is "Take intelligent risks."

At the heart of this is that we will be wrong sometimes, but as long as we go into our decisions with the best information available at the time, it is not just okay to fail, it's required to happen from time to time. If we never fail, we are not pushing ourselves far enough. A corollary is that it is impossible to learn if we do not first accept that we don't know everything.

Let's tackle first the unfortunate pressure on people to feel like they have all the answers. All too often in meetings we see someone tap dancing nervously around an answer that they don't have—which often happens when asked a question by someone higher up the management chain. We've all been there, afraid to look underprepared or inadequate.

It invariably results in one of two outcomes. The questioner can request the person to find the answer and follow up later, which encourages the behavior we want to see and makes it okay not to know. A worse alternative is if they just accept the given answer as correct, which frequently ends up propagating bad information that might be found out later.

Why can't someone just flat out say they don't have the answer? Because they feel those present will often lose confidence in the person answering this honestly. But what exactly is wrong with not knowing an answer?

Upon reflection, I think we have forgotten that it is not our role as engineers and leaders always to have the answers. It is far more important to know how to find the answers than it is to have them ready at hand. An answer of, "I don't know, but I will find out and get back to you," demonstrates that you can be trusted to provide an informed view. It means that when you do have an answer at hand, it's not because you made it up on the spot.

Now, what happens if you answer incorrectly? A culture where being able to say "I don't know," I believe, actually normalizes the ability to be wrong. If you were wrong because you made the first answer up and were scared to admit you didn't know, and then someone else points out the flaw later, you lose credibility over time.

However, if you were wrong because you answered with the best information available at the time, but have prefaced that you don't know, then you are known to always give informed answers and not provide an answer you don't have information for—you show that you can learn and grow as a technologist.

I have worked in companies where it was not okay to be wrong or not have the answers. Places where politics were far more prevalent. The difference is in another of LinkedIn's values, "Be open, honest, and constructive." Cultivating an open culture, one in which we do not assign blame but instead seek to understand, means that we can be vulnerable with each other with the understanding that it will not be used against us later.

Our industry frequently talks about blameless retrospectives, but it's critical to bring that to all aspects of our work. When we or our colleagues fall, we need to help each other back up and move forward together with the knowledge we have gained. Growth means risk, and risk means sometimes we are wrong. Otherwise, we stagnate.

Storytelling Is a Superpower

Anita Clarke

Shopify

Upon learning my job title would be Engineering Storyteller, I knew I was jumping into some Silicon Valley realness (even though I was in Toronto). It was the Valleyest of titles I'd ever heard—and I've heard some hilarious ones over the years. I chuckled when I told people; wouldn't you? Only after my first story was published did I understand that the title was a brilliant distillation of my role.

So what is an engineering storyteller? Storytelling is a tradition passed down through the millennia, and it has survived because we are built to consume, create, and process the world through stories. Part of my role is to help SREs create smart and engaging technical stories and to find a home for them, whether they are written down in blog posts or told orally through presentations and podcasts.

When I do my job well, something unlocks in the world, and an explosion of excitement pours out from the sharing of information. I'm no longer surprised by the reaction. After all, great storytelling is a superpower that shows you're engaged and passionate about the work you're doing. It shows you have empathy for your peers and want to make collaboration and learning easier. Most important, it shows that not only do you want to share your ideas; you want people to understand them also.

A common misconception exists that working in a technical field means that you won't need to interact with people or develop so-called soft skills. I bought into it too when I first got into software development, thinking I could deal with machines all day. My first couple of jobs drove home that that belief was a fallacy.

I realized the commonalities with my former life as an athlete: teams that communicate clearly, quickly, and effectively are superior to those of otherwise equal skills. A star player on a team is only able to be a star through the support and alignment with the rest of the team, and so it goes for the team at work.

Storytelling especially matters in SRE because the work that's being done can seem mystical to other teams. How exactly are you diagnosing the system, and what exactly is happening? You have to be able to share in a way that makes sense for other teams. Storytelling brings a greater depth of knowledge to your work and, hopefully, new insights and ideas.

To unlock this power, you must practice, practice, practice. Writing and crafting narratives about your ideas takes time and lots of iterations. The skill of writing is built, not born. It isn't just about the words you're using; it's about breaking down complex topics in a way your audience understands.

Here's how you can intentionally be a great storyteller:

Be clear and concise
Use accessible language and be direct.

Be detailed
Brevity isn't always your friend; your decisions and process are as important as the results.

Show your receipts
Back up your claims with proof, but don't editorialize the results.

Be helpful
It's about the reader, not an ego trip.

Speak the reader's language
Ideas need to be understood, so share in a way best suited to your audience.

Storytelling has a home with SRE, especially given the stories you share about memorable outages and incidents, but you can use it beyond recalling horror and hero stories. Storytelling perfects communication skills, establishes expertise, creates essential professional networking opportunities, helps solve problems, and increases confidence. It's a superpower, but one you can manifest.

Get Your Work Recognized: Write a Brag Document

Julia Evans and Karla Burnett

Wizard Zines
Stripe

There's this idea that if you do great work at your job, people will automatically recognize that and reward you with promotions and increased pay. This isn't always true! Your manager certainly doesn't remember everything important you did, and if you reflect on it, even *you* probably don't remember everything you've done in the past year.

Here's a simple tactic that can help you get your work recognized: *write a document listing your accomplishments*. Instead of trying to remember it all, maintain your brag document, which lists everything so you can refer to it when you get to performance review season!

Here's an example structure:

- *Goals for this year* (Have you been really focused on security? On building a culture of code review on your team?)
- *Goals for next year*
- *Projects* (Explain your contributions and their impact to your company. Numbers are good!)
- *Mentoring and leadership work* (Include community building and glue work.)
- *Design and documentation* (Keep design docs and documentation you wrote!)
- *What you learned*
- *Outside of work* (Talks! Blog posts!)

This document can be quite comprehensive if you want; 10 bulleted pages for a year of work isn't too much, especially with graphs or screenshots. You can write it all at once or update a running list weekly; just keep it structured so that a reader can find what they're looking for easily.

Stick to the facts. When we came up with this idea at Stripe, we called it a brag document because many people feel uncomfortable talking about the work they've done, even if it's excellent. ("It feels like bragging!") If that sounds like you, it's okay to write down your accomplishments, even if it's a little uncomfortable at first.

Don't try to make your work sound better than it is, though; just make it sound *exactly as good as it is,* for example, "was the primary contributor to X new feature that's now used by 60% of our customers and has gotten Y positive feedback." Where possible, link out to sources for how you came up with a number; it's hard to argue with facts!

Share your brag document. You might feel self-conscious at first, sharing your brag document with your manager. But every single manager we've spoken to LOVES when their reports share a brag document with them. It makes writing your performance review way easier and it means they have all the facts on hand when they're advocating for you to be promoted. Brag documents also *really* help with manager transitions, for example, if you get a new manager 3 months before a performance review cycle.

Similarly, share your brag document with your coworkers! If they're writing peer feedback for you at performance time, having a list of what you've worked on and your goals makes it much easier to see the areas you want feedback on. Outside of performance time, sharing your doc helps your peers understand what you're aiming for and how they can help. We've gotten offers for introductions to conference organizers and suggestions for project ideas after writing down related goals.

Look for patterns. Brag documents also help you reflect on the work you've done. Reading over them can help you understand what work you feel proud of, what you wish you were doing more or less of, what you could do better next time, and the longer-term impact of projects you worked on years ago.

They help others too: when you do get promoted, you can share your historical brag documents with people you're mentoring, to explain the path you took and make that promotion seem more attainable for the next person.

PART III

One to Ten

Making Work Visible

Lorin Hochstein

Netflix

Wait a second. . .you used a REPL[1] to figure it out?

I was taking notes for a colleague who was interviewing an engineer after an incident. One particular service had gotten stuck, and the engineer was discussing how they figured out what the problem was. Before that moment, I had no idea that we supported launching a REPL on a production box to interrogate the state of that service.

Most of the work that we do is invisible to others; they see the results, but not how we got there. Even during an incident, where we're working in close collaboration with others, our peers rarely have the opportunity to observe exactly what we're doing. They don't see which queries we're running, which graphs or logs we're looking at, how we interpret these results, and how we decide where to look next.

There is enormous value in *making this work visible*: in providing coworkers with a window into the messy details of our day-to-day work.

In order to address the problems people encounter in our organizations, we need to understand what those problems are: an operational tool has an error-prone user interface, or a team with a high workload that requires them to constantly context switch.

Nobody in your organization has a complete understanding of how the system works, and we are often bitten by an important bit of context that we didn't have. Although a complete understanding of our systems is unattainable, by seeing the work of others, we can learn more about how the system works. I've learned about all sorts of operator interfaces I never even knew existed.

There's no better way to improve at a skill than direct experience. However, we can also learn from the experiences of others if we have the opportunity

---

1 REPL stands for read-eval-print-loop, an interactive environment.

to watch them in action. The REPL anecdote at the beginning of this essay is a great example.

How do you learn from the experts inside of your organization? In general, the best way to facilitate skill transfer is to watch experts in action. Ideally, you're working alongside them. Watch them solve real problems and document how they mitigated operational surprises: you see how they interpret signals, which tools they use, and you ask them how to make their decisions.

My favorite approach to making work visible is by telling stories. We humans seem to be wired for listening to stories, especially those that contain tension and drama. And there's no better source of tension and drama than incidents!

When we treat incidents as an opportunity to make work visible, this radically changes what our post-incident write-ups look like. The focus of these write-ups shifts from preventive action items to narrative description. We're now writing a story of how the incident unfolded over time, from the perspectives of the different engineers who were engaged. By documenting our incidents using a narrative structure, we can harness the power of storytelling to make work visible in a way that's compelling to the reader.

A good narrative description describes what was going through people's minds in the moment. Think back to the last incident you were involved in. What signals were you receiving that gave them a clue that something was wrong? What led you to look at a particular dashboard or error log that gave you that signal? How did your understanding of what was happening evolve during the incident, and how was it shaped by the later signals you received? How did people coordinate?

Narrative-style write ups take longer to write and longer to read. But, if the narrative is written well, people will happily read the whole thing. They'll learn more about your system than they ever would from a traditional root cause analysis.

An Overlooked Engineering Skill

Murali Suriar

Google

Let me tell you about the time I was on call for 100 different services.

How did this happen? My team was responsible for connecting to various network services run by other companies. The services ran on top of the same physical infrastructure but were otherwise extremely diverse. Routing protocols, application protocols, firewall rules—everything was different.

One day I might handle a request for new access to an existing service, the next, debug an application by going through several firewalls and NAT (network address translation) devices on a service commissioned the previous month by a contractor who had moved on to another job. In an ideal world, the person with the most context would be on call when that service breaks. The world is not ideal.

Failing that, what did we do? Diagrams. If you ask someone to draw a diagram representing a system, you get insight into how they think about that system.

Ask two people on your team to draw an overview diagram of a system your team owns and then compare the two diagrams. The similarities and differences in the diagrams will likely reveal something about the mental models that each team member is using when interacting with the system. Diagrams are a communication tool, but more than that, they are a tool for recording and sharing mental models. Their greatest power is not in what they display but in how they express and shape people's thinking about systems.

Once a mental model can be recorded, reproduced, and shared, it becomes a general-purpose abstraction. It speeds communication and gives people standard tools they can refer to when reasoning about behavior, outages, and proposed changes to the system. Even if the abstractions are not strictly accurate, when most of a team shares the same mental model of a system, that system's behavior will evolve to match the model over time.

Following in the footsteps of other network engineers, we applied their conventions for drawing diagrams at different layers (physical, data link, network, routing, and security policy) and even for some de facto standards for icons for devices to our infrastructure and the services we ran. We had a standard diagram of our physical infrastructure. The full version consisted of nine pairs of devices; it could be reduced to five pairs of devices or five single logical devices, depending on what level of detail was needed. Each of these diagrams could be drawn from memory by anyone on the team.

We then created variants of these standard diagrams for each service, overlaid with specific details. When paged for an unfamiliar service, I was able to orient myself quickly and understand how the service was structured.

Whenever I join a team, I look for their diagrams to help understand the system's abstractions. If no one can teach me meaningful abstractions, then I just draw what exists and try to use those diagrams to find abstractions and models to aid my understanding.

So how do I go about doing this?

- If I start with some simple abstractions, I build a diagram for each one.
- If I start with diagrams, I think about which ones provide useful mental models.
- If I start with nothing, I just draw what exists and see what patterns and structures I find.

Remember, the goal is not necessarily 100% accuracy. Prioritize humans: the diagrams and abstractions should be memorable and useful and should remain current over time. Humans, after all, will be the ones using your diagrams, whether for reference (like the preceding service diagrams) or for study.

Unpacking the On-Call Divide

Jason Hand

Microsoft

Disagreements about just *who* should be responsible for the on-call role have always been a cornerstone irritation of my professional career. The arguments are all valid and the reasoning is sound. Yet despite all the logical and fair points, engaging in the debate remains a contentious effort.

Predictably, once everyone has had an opportunity to share their points and personal stories, a truce is made, relenting that the answer to the question of who should be on call for a digital service is, "It *depends*."

It depends on a multitude of scenarios and considerations, all of which are unique not only to industries but across businesses and teams within organizations. Countless flavors of on call exist because the scenarios in which on call is a necessity are limitless.

But here's the thing: the olive branch statement, "it depends," doesn't really solve or end the debate, nor does it get to the heart of why the argument persists. When you unpack the rationale behind strongly held feelings and opinions on the subject, you have to ask why we feel the need to continue to raise the question of who should be on call. What problem is that solving?

Regardless of which side of the DevOps bimodal view of the world you fall in, how systems are designed, built, and operated vary greatly, but most people agree on two important points: the on-call role is a necessity, and most would rather not do it.

We all have scars from this thing, but for the debate to conclude, our personal experience of being on call must first be recognized and acknowledged. Each and every one of our experiences is valid and indeed important institutional knowledge of the collective understanding of what it's like to be on call.

My experiences. Your experiences. They all represent a higher-fidelity picture and understanding about what took place, more than any log or metric can—that is, if your goal is to improve the on-call role in a way that addresses what truly bothers us about it. The personal realities of what took place and the quality of the human impact are what we want to improve.

It's easy to implement tools to help us minimize the business impact. Yay! The board and stockholders will be pleased. But did we do anything to improve the on-call experience for our future self and for those who will follow?

This is the *problem* to solve, and it starts by providing the time and space to share and listen, to explore what's going on cognitively before, during, and after responding to problems and, unfortunately, that data doesn't show up in transcripts, system logs, or time series data that we typically spend the most attention on during a retrospective analysis.

So far, we haven't found a meaningful way to include acknowledgment and exploration in the mental calisthenics people go through as well as their cognitive reasoning, judgment, and decision-making mechanics in our retrospective exercises.

However, to resolve the on-call divide, we need to start exploring the gap between us. *What was it like to be on call?* Asking what happened, in the hopes of understanding why so that we can prevent it, is no more than a topical medicine for a deeper problem; much more hides beneath the scar.

If we can look below the surface, we'll find that with a little extra time and effort, the irritations of being on call can be minimized and the divide narrowed simply by creating the space and safety to reveal a more complete picture of what happened while we were on call.

The Maestros of Incident Response

Andrew Louis

DigitalOcean

We've all been there: the first time we're the IMOC (Incident Manager On-Call, or Incident Commander, others might call it). My first IMOC page hit a year into the gig and, regardless of all the observing I did before, my handling of it paled compared to the performances before mine. It wasn't my last fumble, but I began to build a high-level framework for incident management. With each fumble that followed, I added something new to it. The framework has remained valuable as a starting point, and I hope it will be helpful to you too.

There is more and better material dedicated to expanding how to manage an incident, but here are the primary principles that I keep at the forefront.

Stop the Bleeding

Keep the focus unrelentingly on prioritizing mitigation. Although the conversation might drift into deep root-cause investigations and discussions of longer-term solutions, the first impulse should be to keep the ongoing conversation focused solely on recovering the current situation.

What's Everyone Doing?

At regular intervals (be wary of the cost this could impose on folks working on the problem), continue to raise the question of what everyone is doing. The goal here will be to keep track of the efforts, prevent overlapping work from going on, and get health checks from the parties involved.

Raising this question also gives you the opportunity to ask another—Do you need any help?—to gauge whether more resources should be leveraged.

As you work through the incident management process, it might not be obvious when to move to a next step. Perhaps you could be a bit more certain about which systems are affected if you spent an extra five minutes gathering some more data points. In this scenario, always optimize for speed over quality as you make your decisions, keeping the big-picture goal in mind: to recover your systems fast.

At this point, you might realize that a lot of working through incident response boils down to building the muscle memory and neural pathways that come from repeated experience, but that doesn't mean you can't prepare for the rotation.

Here's a little starter preparedness checklist:

- What are the organization's key metrics? In an e-commerce organization, this may be checkout rate and volume, storefront availability, and so on.
- Do you have a sense of how to index from services to owners?
- Are you able to get a sense of the ongoing alerts going off across the organization?

Regardless, all the frameworks in the world won't prepare you nearly enough for the first time you'll lead an incident. My first hit around 4 a.m. in Toronto and my performance felt like the Chernobyl of incident management. In a seat formerly warmed by maestros, I was a clumsy, amateur conductor.

A lot of working through incident response boils down to building muscle memory and neural pathways that come from repeated experience. Over the many pages that followed, with patience and practice, I started to fumble less and less and soon started getting the orchestra to play some bops.

Effortless Incident Management

Suhail Patel,
Miles Bryant,
and Chris Evans

Monzo

Humans are one of the most important factors in incident management processes, and that's no different for incidents that SREs will become involved in. Managed incorrectly, an incident can have too many parallel conflicting streams (individuals stepping on top of each other) or not enough collaboration (individuals trying to resolve the incident on their own). Here are the key steps to achieve effortless incident management

The first thing to do in all incidents is *nominate an incident lead* and make it clear to everyone in the incident who the lead is at all times. This is the individual tasked with coordinating the roles and responsibilities of everyone involved in the incident and delegating tasks. The incident lead doesn't have to be the person most familiar with the systems affected; rather, it can be someone who can bring the right groups of people together. The lead does not need to remain static throughout the incident; another individual can take on the incident lead role once they've gained all the context needed.

Consider *setting up a dedicated incident communication channel* (in your chat software) for each incident. A dedicated channel breaks down any existing silos such as existing organizational team structures and communication boundaries in favor of a new shared objective of everyone coming together to resolve the incident at hand. As a bonus, a dedicated channel can serve as a linear timeline of an incident as it unfolds. This can aid massively when it's time to write an incident report.

It's important for everyone involved to *take the time to describe clearly what they've found* and avoid ambiguity. The time taken for you to vocalize findings seems at odds with continuing to investigate the actual incident; however, it can provide an implicit set of added validation. Examples of this are things like explaining about sharing the output of commands or surfacing documentation about a system that others may not be as familiar with.

During an incident, you may encounter additional things that aren't as intended (such as broken dashboards or out-of-date runbooks). *Log follow-up actions during incidents*, rather than waiting until the end, so they are not forgotten. Once the incident is over, the incident lead can evaluate the proposed action list and assign owners for the actions you decide to keep.

Incident response is a flurry of actions. Automation can help reduce the overhead. We built a tool called Response to help reduce the pressure and cognitive burden on individuals during an incident and steer everyone through the incident management process in a unified way. Response gives a step-by-step flow to log an incident with a lead, start a dedicated communication channel, escalate in another team, and log actions, all without leaving Slack (our preferred chat software at Monzo).

We spent a lot of time making the user experience of Response, for declaring and managing incidents, as frictionless as possible. All incidents are automatically cataloged in a dedicated Slack channel by Response on creation. Each incident displays the title, severity, incident lead, and Slack channel front and center.

Building tooling and processes around incidents isn't everything, though. Those involved in an incident need to have the cultural safety to *communicate effectively without distraction, judgment, or prejudice* on their abilities. Incidents and their retrospective debriefs should be free from finger-pointing or assignment of blame. Having an effective incident management process revolves around having both the right tooling and the right cultural attitude toward resolving the incident at hand.

The incident management process doesn't need to be a burden. Done correctly, *incidents can be powerful lessons* for everyone on how systems work together, gather trust and empathy from other peers, and showcase the agility and collaborative nature of an entire organization.

If You're Doing Runbooks, Do Them Well

Spike Lindsey

Shopify

Runbooks (also known as playbooks) are not a silver bullet (nothing is), and yet a common action item after an incident is "update runbooks/add missing runbooks." So why do we persist?

Runbooks are generally concerned with known unknowns, and we cannot anticipate every problem. They share all of documentation's pitfalls: accuracy, quality, maintainability, drift. They are relied on in time-pressured, stressful situations. They can sometimes be a fragile bandage over reliability issues: instead of investing in fixing underlying issues, teams overinvest in runbooks, creating new sources of toil. They can be seen as direct substitutes for training and experience, resulting in situations in which newer or less-experienced team members are put on call for systems that they don't yet understand, simply because "runbooks exist." Inaccurate or outdated runbooks can sometimes be more dangerous than no runbooks.

From that brief list, you might think that I am deeply opposed to runbooks—quite the opposite. As with any system, understanding the downsides means that we can work to mitigate or fix them and benefit better from the upsides.

Runbook creation, maintenance, and review should be a whole-team activity. Recognizing that runbooks are a solution to a knowledge distribution problem (rather than a technical problem) can facilitate writing them, especially when done in a collaborative way. Runbooks capture the thought process and decision making of a team member who knows how to fix a problem. Some possible questions for that team member are: What are you using to determine whether there is a problem? What tools do you reach for? What feeds into your decision process? Are any actions dangerous or risky? What parts of this process have tripped you up before and that you'd recommend taking extra care doing? Periodically reviewing runbooks as a team also allows this knowledge to be reviewed and questioned, especially as systems evolve.

Runbooks are technical debt. They are often the only useful documentation of a system's technical debt and toil. (The cards loitering at the bottom of backlogs don't count.) When reviewing an existing runbook, teams should question why it exists and whether it can be eliminated. By this logic, having too many runbooks is an anti-pattern. Seeing runbooks as cross-system orchestration (with humans as the controller) may also help understand what can and can't be easily automated away, or whether there's a missing control system.

The worst time to read or run a runbook for the first time is in the middle of the night, during an incident. Think of fire extinguishers or smoke alarms: they need to be regularly tested to make sure that they will work when needed in an emergency. This includes checking that links and code snippets actually work. Keeping a record of when a runbook was last used or tested and running through stale ones also provides an opportunity to assess continuously whether that runbook is still needed.

Runbooks cannot and will not solve every incident. But that's fine; as systems grow in complexity, teams mature, and incidents become more novel, there is a point at which an investment in runbooks starts to show diminishing returns. In the short term, this may mean an evolution in the runbooks' focus, either toward signposting of useful resources and diagnostic techniques or toward a more minimalist approach: isolate/terminate/cycle what's broken, and if that doesn't work, escalate.

In the long term, creating a healthy culture and process around runbooks—in other words, a culture based on knowledge sharing, collaboration, leveling up, and preparation—can have a better payoff than even the runbooks themselves. If you're doing runbooks, do them well.

Why I Hate Our Playbooks

Frances Rees

Google

Playbooks (also known as runbooks) in SRE are collections of documentation intended to help an on-caller resolve issues. There are many styles of playbooks, but most that I've encountered suffer from the same antipatterns.

First, they can contain too much detail, making them difficult to maintain and creating large documents, which complicates finding specific information. This is often caused by a fear of missing anything. Examples of such playbooks are those written during a transfer of on-call ownership or as a continuous log by on-callers.

It's infeasible to assume that any playbook is absolutely complete, so it's important to expect it to be a tool that cannot fill the entire role of an SRE. The content covered in team onboarding is a useful baseline for the level of detail that can be elided as assumed knowledge. It's also beneficial to replace details, such as how to locate a job with links, to speed up data search without requiring recall of myriad small facts. A special case to consider is playbooks written for users and customers of an infrastructure service, as opposed to those written for the owners of the service, for whom a very different level of background knowledge is needed. Caveats and unintuitive implications can easily cause accidental harm to users.

The opposite can happen with too little detail. Well-meaning requirements for documentation, but without incentives for spending time to make it useful, lead to empty templates. Too little detail actually wastes more time than being able to see that no documentation exists, so a minimum level of viability is needed on submission. At best, an empty document isn't useful, but at worst, it can foster a pattern of ignoring the playbooks (even if they're updated), because the on caller has internalized that they aren't useful.

It sounds counterintuitive, but playbooks should not be written by experts on the topic. It's often difficult for people very familiar with a system to identify the context and subtleties that only they know, so they are better suited to be information sources and reviewers.

The last anti-pattern is that of being too prescriptive. Any playbook that can describe the exact steps to resolve an exact circumstance should be an automated script instead. An alert should mean that the system can't fix itself, because automation is much faster and much better at fully enumerated repetitive tasks than humans. We escalate to humans for a complex response, not a fast response.

If on-callers are conditioned to follow a script, novel events also become very difficult to handle, which is a problem because they're the ideal environment for SREs in our continuing mission to automate ourselves out of a job. It's important to recognize that playbooks have a life cycle:

```
┌->1 Identify issue
|  2 Debug
|  3 Add alerts
|  4 Write documentation
| ┌>5 Automate resolution
| └-6 Update documentation
└--7 Have a different problem
```

We *very often* get stuck at #4. Prescriptive playbooks aren't a failure that should be deleted, but they're an opportunity to automate and iterate.

Ideally, a playbook should only contain:

1. Why do I care? Severity and qualification of the user-visible impact.

2. What can I look at? Consoles, logs, and inspection tools.

3. What can I do? Mitigation tooling.

4. Whom can I escalate to? Developers, back-end teams, or a dedicated incident response team.

Good playbooks at their heart reflect the SRE culture to which we aspire. They rely on providing the right incentives not only to document but to automate and innovate. Identifying and focusing on the goals of the team helps refine useful information for navigating the uncertainty that makes our job interesting and avoiding the tedium.

What Machines Do Well

Michelle Brush

Google

One common approach to building automation is to have a human do the manual process, capture it, and then create a script that reproduces the human's workflow. It seems reasonable—so what's wrong with it? This approach doesn't consider what steps required a decision that only a human could make, and it doesn't recognize that a computer might be able to do some things better.

Understanding what humans and machines do well is essential to building good automation.

To automate a complex process, we need to evaluate which aspects of it require human interpretation and reaction. This usually means looking for places it could fail. If some command executed or service call returns an error, we should consider what the human would do at that time and compare that to what the machine could do. Can we replicate the same decision-making process in code? If so, we should. If not, we can fail the automation and alert a human to come make the right decision. For really complex and costly decisions, keeping a human in the process sometimes makes sense.

Another option is to redesign this step so it doesn't require a human. Automation engineering may require revisiting the design and interfaces of systems it will automate, because there are design principles that make it easier for machines to decide and act. If the system being automated doesn't adhere to the principles, the automation is likely to be fragile—and fragile automation needs human supervision.

Idempotency, the property of an operation that allows it to be repeated without side effects, is key to automation. If something fails or fails to return a success in a timely manner, the automation can retry it without consequence. This is a design principle that allows automation to be resilient. When possible, we should favor making the commands and services being called by automation idempotent.

Consistent and codified error reporting is another property of systems that allows for better automation. If humans have to do deep troubleshooting or interpret strings to understand what happens when something fails, the automation will fail and require humans to intervene. Automation should also avoid relying on parsing or matching descriptive strings, because it creates a risk that things will break if those strings change or similar strings are added.Consider also that systems being automated need the ability to scale. Tools and APIs (application programming interfaces) built for human interaction may not keep pace with the speed a machine can execute. The underlying system may need to be load tested and improved to meet the demands of the automation.

Automation is often composed of other automation. We should expect our automation one day to be part of a larger system. This means the automation we build should meet the same aforementioned properties. We should make the automation idempotent. We should have it use consistent and codified error reporting, and we should make sure it can scale. We should also have tests and documentation. We should monitor it, just like the rest of the system.

The more we make automation like any other software we'd develop—meaning carefully designed, tested, monitored, and documented—the more it becomes something we can safely rely on.

Integrating Empathy into SRE Tools

Daniella Niyonkuru

Shopify

Site reliability engineering includes best practices such as building self-healing services, implementing automatic systems, and watching the quality and quantity of on-call shifts. Yet, we hardly have tools for site reliability engineers that promote self-healing from operational exhaustion, relieve incident-related stress, and track on-call rotations.

Compassionate empathy can help us reach this objective by acting on the elements that make burnout more likely to occur. Building compassionate empathy into software requires understanding (and sometimes collecting) the elements that are often at the center of SRE distress and encoding-related alleviation measures.

These steps support integrating an empathetic approach:

1. Understand the source.
2. Find the right metrics (SLIs).
3. Fix an acceptable range (SLOs).
4. Draw the consequences (SLAs).
5. Implement tooling to track SLIs, check SLOs, and enforce SLAs.

Let's illustrate these steps with an example. Shuri is an SRE at SuperSonicSystems, and a year ago her team was revamped along with their on-call rotation. This resulted in her taking stress leave. Let's apply our approach to ensure that this does not happen to the rest of the SRE team.

To understand the source, an investigative survey was sent to Shuri. The results show that she was on call more often and encountered numerous alerts, making it hard to recuperate. This happened because the on-call rotation previously handled by nine people was reduced to three. Although the systems were divided by the manager, extracted incident response data shows that Shuri was on call more often and received more pages as her shifts coincided with the company's release week. In addition, the company's on-call policy does not offer recovery days.

The quantity and quality of on-call shifts were the main culprits. The three metrics the organization focuses on are:

- On-call frequency (How many people and how often are they on call?)
- Alerts per shift (How many alerts do SREs get per shift?)
- SRE happiness (What's the happiness level of SREs after their on-call shift?)

From these SLIs, SuperSonicSystems picked some SLOs.

On-call rotation
A minimum of eight people should be in the rotation, assuming week-long shifts and a primary/secondary setup.

Alerts per shift
The maximum of 10 alerts per shift, with nighttime alerts carrying double the weight. In the future, higher-severity alerts might also be associated with a higher weight.

SRE happiness
A survey using an emoji rating is sent to SREs after each on call, with the goal to have an average of ☺. This is different from the previous SLOs in that it is qualitative instead of quantitative.

This step requires trial and error until a comfortable balance is achieved.

The last step is setting the consequences, or SLAs.

On-call rotation
If the upper range is not respected, teams should staff their on-call rotation with more people to make this sustainable. In a transitory phase, people who are more often on call will get two mandatory consecutive days of recovering to prevent burnout.

Alerts per shift
If the maximum number of alerts has been attained, the pager will be taken by someone else on the team to allow proper time for recovering.

SRE happiness
A survey below the average rating will prompt a follow-up and potentially related actions. For instance, an SRE who is going through a rough

life patch could be taken off the rotation for a while. These cases should be individually analyzed by team leads.

SREs must support companies' most critical systems, but the elements that make the role exciting and challenging also put them at risk of burnout, health issues, and discontentment. This example shows how empathy can be integrated into an on-call policy for stronger, more resilient teams.

Using ChatOps to Implement Empathy

Daniella Niyonkuru

Shopify

"Janet is handling an incident lasting over an hour. Another available commander should offer to hand off or override the rest of their shift so Janet can take a break!"

This addition to our ChatOps incident response reminder sequence sounded so simple at first, yet it wasn't long after that I observed how impactful it was to SREs who were on call. The two-sentence prompt led available commanders to reach out right away and offer to help—and this gesture seemed to reinvigorate the on-call commander.

That's when I realized that ChatOps, beyond automating and offering an easy interface to manage incident response and infrastructure, also has the power to make our work more sustainable.

SRE teams are often overworked due to the nature of their work. The focus can be so much on systems that the SREs behind them are forgotten. Dealing with too much toil, having night shifts, and constantly being the first line of defense against outages can take a toll on SREs and consequently the systems they work on. In Integrating Empathy into SRE Tools, page 90, I discuss how implementing empathy is important and can alleviate the burden, but given that teams are also resource- and time-limited, how best to implement it?

We look to a trusted tool in the SRE toolkit: automation. After doing the difficult work of creating the boundaries, limits, and budgets for empathetic work, using ChatOps is a great way to ensure that they can be implemented without requiring constant observation. ChatOps is all about conversation-driven operations and uses group chat tools to go beyond basic conversation with context and actions taken from within the chat tool itself. This helps build in empathy and automate actions that will prevent burnout and exhaustion.

The introductory example shows how this works: by tracking the elapsed time since the beginning of the incident and sending an automated reminder to the commanders' Slack channel. It hence automatically prompts a reaction from other commanders who would otherwise be unaware of the situation.

Similarly, ChatOps can serve as a safeguard for on-calls' quantity and quality. Communication between the chatbot and third-party services (PagerDuty, Datadog, and so on) is usually done by webhooks. By implementing on-call scheduling commands, a chatbot can, in response, validate the sustainability of the desired schedule against set gold standards.

For instance, a new manager who would attempt to change the schedule to have only three engineers when the minimum is eight could see the bot reject their request and nudge them to follow best practice. As for tracking on-call quality, a chatbot can automatically send a survey after each shift and help track the team morale. It can also prompt SREs to take time off when they have encountered particularly stressful on calls.

By tracking the number and severity of incidents, a chatbot can let the SRE know that they have an on-call recoup day or are off for the rest of their shift. By tracking the quantity and quality of on-call through tools that extract schedules' data and alerts, ChatOps ensures even load among the team and is essential to prevent burnout. Not only does it help sustain SREs, it can provide management with useful data to spot problems early and fix blind spots.

The examples presented here demonstrate that ChatOps can be used to maintain a healthy team by exploiting the power of automation. It prevents time otherwise spent tracking elements manually and improves adherence to set budgets.

Move Fast to Unbreak Things

Michelle Brush

Google

As SREs, we see our job as balancing velocity with reliability. We know each change deployed to production, whether code or configuration, carries some risk of causing an outage or other degradation of service. When an outage happens, our immediate reaction is to be more cautious, to slow down production changes.

Then things still break. Despite our efforts, there are still outages. Our instinct was wrong. Things are now more likely to break *exactly* because we slowed down. When a plane stalls in midair, the natural reaction might be to pull up, to pull away from the ground. The right answer is to point the nose of the plane down and increase engine power. This generates lift. Sometimes the right thing to do is the opposite of what our intuition tells us.

Your development organization is a faucet. It produces change (whether features, bugs, or architectural work) at a somewhat constant rate. Separately, there's a rate at which those changes can flow into production. The production flow rate is determined by your deployment cadence, the speed of your quality assurance process, any approval requirements, and so on.

What happens when you slow that cadence, whether explicitly by freezing or implicitly through increased review, human checks, or a change approval process? You accumulate a bigger backlog of changes awaiting deployment. Production looks less and less like your testing environments. Each additional change batched into your deployment increases the odds something goes wrong.

With this increased risk, inevitably, you deploy and things still break. What do you do? The first and obvious answer is to roll back. That's a great answer. However, if you've deployed as a batch of changes, you have to roll all of them back: bug fixes, features, and all. Some of those changes deployed with the bug might be critical needs for your users.

Say instead of rolling back, you mitigate the immediate concern and then want to fix the issue. That fix now needs to go through all the tests, reviews, and controls you introduced, delaying mitigation.

In the long term, the intuitive reaction to production breakage prolongs breakages. This isn't to say you should move fast because you're going to break things anyway. You want your qualification and release process to be robust. It should also be fast. You will achieve better outcomes by giving people the levers and buttons they need to respond and repair the system quickly.

Deploy what's ready as soon as it's ready. Then trust it. You can achieve this with continuous delivery. If you're not there yet, you can approach it through a regular, frequent, and decreasing deployment cadence: weekly to daily, daily to hourly, and so on. Your deployment still carries the cumulative risk of all the changes packed into it, but you've constrained that risk to changes produced in the time period you selected.

Once the flow of changes coming from the development organization matches the flow of changes into production, the gap between your mental model of the system and the actual system shrinks. Things become easier to detect and fix.

When you still have outages, as you will, and your gut tells you to slow down, consider slowing the rate of feature development work, not the deployment of it. Shift engineering efforts to improving system observability or faster tests. Build improved tools for quickly mitigating outages: rollback automation, failover tooling, and so on. Invest in those long overdue architectural improvements. Also, realize that even these changes should be deployed to production incrementally and often.

The key to reliability is the ability to make the system better quickly. Anything that slows down change slows your ability to do this as well.

You Don't Know for Sure Until It Runs in Production

Ingrid Epure

Netlify

The idea of testing in production is usually met with two types of reactions. Sometimes you get enthusiastic YAYs! Other times, you might get shocked, disapproving looks.

What explains this divide? This is one of the most interesting paradoxes of engineering. We often view production as this house of cards–like, fragile ecosystem that needs to be approached with care, silk gloves, or bunker gear. At the same time, we dream of observable systems and peaceful, pager-free nights.

Spoiler alert, you can't have it both ways. So how do we bridge this gap?

For one, we must confront the myth that absolutely, under no circumstances, should bugs ever reach production. The idea of viewing shipped code as an experiment somehow implies that it's not done or scrappy and that iterating while shipping is somehow bad.

You may feel that you can't test in production because of a lack of good tooling. The bravest organizations attempt to build tools in-house, yet without a unified standard of running production experiments for the rest of us, that usually means scraping some Bash script together in the little time left between feature work sessions—or, even worse, making it an "ops problem."

However, it's far from an all-or-nothing approach; instead, it's a sum of small things that can fundamentally change the developer experience, some of which you might already be doing!

There's feature flagging, which allows modifying system behavior without changing code.

There's tooling to access production data safely or interact with your application from the command line. Whether you love or hate Rails doesn't change that the console is amazing for debugging, and many frameworks and languages can take a page from that book.

There are libraries that help with refactoring and migrating legacy systems by running old code paths alongside new ones, comparing results and even performance!

There is also observability, or heavily relying on events and distributed traces rather than on traditionally fixed metrics. In other words, instrument the code to craft a story about the systems rather than provide fixed information, and have it answer dynamic, complex questions.

However, this isn't just about tooling; it is also a chance to start viewing initial production code as an experiment. Think of it as the first pancake to test whether your griddle is at the right temperature. You can always adjust for the next one. Imagine a shift in mindset in which we make observations and draw conclusions to understand better how our systems work, and the impact of our changes at scale, in a real-life environment. It involves shipping in smaller iterations, which increases the likelihood of catching really bad edge cases early, and mitigating them quickly, making production less scary and *final*.

Production transforms into an avenue of creativity and trust by providing much-needed confidence in your system and changes you've just made. It also means sleeping better at night, knowing your code has a lower risk of running into unknown bugs that could take days to fix.

And couldn't we all use a little more peace and sleep?

Sometimes the Fix Is the Problem

Jake Pittis

Stripe

If simpler systems fail less and are faster to restore, why do incident reviews focus so much on adding fixes rather than on removing components and code? When we should be reducing bug surface area and increasing operator understandability, we instead lean toward adding validation, sanity checks, traffic shifting, and synchronization—all things that add complexity. Even just fixing bugs can end up adding extra code and complexity.

Complexity is often justified with the benefits to reliability outweighing the risk of future incidents. At the end of the day, some complexity is necessary for business functionality, just as some complexity is necessary for reliability. But how often do we focus on trying to remove excess complexity?

Incident reviews are a perfect opportunity to target and remove detrimental complexity. Sometimes this can be code that increases bug surface area and sometimes it can be something that makes systems harder to understand and leads to slower incident response. In both cases, if we can show that it contributed to the incident and that it's not necessary for reliability or business functionality, then it should be considered detrimental complexity and be removed.

Incidents give us the space to zoom out and notice detrimental complexity. If a bug leads to an incident, we can ask ourselves whether something about the system made it hard to test or to notice that a bug was present. Maybe it was hiding in some concurrent code. By zooming out more, we can ask whether the functionality provided by the—almost always complex—concurrent code is necessary. Remember to ask the tough questions, such as whether the performance benefits that the concurrency provides are actually a requirement for the system's functionality.

Similarly, to analyze a slow incident response, we can ask whether there was something about the system that confused or misled operators. Maybe it was hard to tell when a piece of configuration was dynamically updated. Now is the time to ask whether the functionality this complexity provides is necessary. For example, could the configuration be made static without sacrificing functionality? Most important, don't forget to consider whether the complexity contributed to past incidents!

Simpler systems that aren't perfect are usually better than complex ones. Immutable data structures allow programmers and operators to avoid tracking state changes and often the performance hit is not noticed. Polling can be less efficient and slower than push-based pipelines but avoids difficult concurrency patterns. The tooling required to maintain a zero-downtime system can be quite involved, much more so than just having regular maintenance windows. Dynamic configuration can be speedy and toil-free, but configuring services statically and forcing a restart is dead easy to understand. Even just having fewer configuration options makes it way more likely that an operator will guess the current state of the system much more accurately.

Every time we add functionality to our system, it brings along some complexity. However, not all complexity is detrimental to reliability. Some is necessary. Because we can't always tell whether the complexity we're adding hinders our future reliability, incident reviews are a perfect time to discuss what role it played. In the end, it's always a trade-off. But I promise, with a little bit of searching, you'll find lots of detrimental complexity during your next incident review!

Legendary

Elise Gale

Microsoft

Why are some outages forgotten as soon as they are mitigated, while others go on to become team legend?

I believe it's because legendary stories follow the hero's journey, a model used in literature to understand a diverse set of tales, from Moses to Harry Potter. Outages, like a hero's journey, have three key parts: the call to action, the road of trials, and the return. I imagine on-call engineers embarking on an epic quest, and following these steps shows us what makes an incident story exciting—and, hopefully, gives us the insight we need to prevent it from happening again.

My legendary call to action begins with, "It was two nights before Christmas. . . ." The timing matters because, frankly, the issue would have been much less interesting any other day of the year, but I was new on the team and had to find the courage, on a company holiday, to page my boss for help.

The road of trials is often the meatiest part—this is when you diagnose and mitigate the situation. This phase is a gold mine for WTF moments. If you are telling your story aloud, this is where your audience should collectively groan. Maybe the log message was missing the one detail you needed to unravel the mystery. Or perhaps, like me, a simple configuration change took six hours and four developers to deploy because of missing tooling.

We discovered the issue was caused by a sister team doing some "harmless" end-of-year cleanup. Luckily, we have matured as a group since then, but I pull out this story anytime someone complains to me about holiday lockdowns or production access security. The lessons from the road of trials are where you should invest your development time to prevent future pain.

The return is important because it has almost nothing to do with our technical systems and everything to do with our team culture. When performing postmortems or root-cause analyses, we often think of incidents in terms of TTx (time to x), as in time to detect or time to mitigate, but these metrics provide us very little insight into what makes an incident interesting. If this is the most interesting part of your story, is it for the right reasons? Or does your team need to work on fostering a blameless culture in which these stories can be shared without judgment?

These legends, whether we mean them to be or not, often live beyond our teams. They are shared at meetups and breweries or, often, during other outages. I learned about the Azure Leap Day outage of 2012 in a recruiting talk at my university. A junior engineer shared his story of writing a code fix in the same conference room as technical fellows and vice presidents. His story demonstrated that you could be involved in important events very early in your career. Ultimately, it shaped my decision to join Microsoft.

Many years and on-call shifts later, I now understand that if an engineer is a hero, there is a gap in the process, the infrastructure, or the tooling. I have also learned that the hero is never alone. After I worked up the courage to call my boss, we figured out the problem together. The four engineers who helped push that configuration change are valued friends and colleagues. And yes, we shared our favorite incidents while we worked.

So gather round, tell your tale, but remember, it isn't all about the hero. It's about the way adversity brings teams together and how we prevent a sequel.

Metrics Are Not SLIs (The Measure Everything Trap)

Brian Murphy

G Research

"Measure everything" is a trap.

It is throwaway advice passed down over time—and no one can rightly recall why. It's the project saddled to the summer intern when immature organizations run out of useful work to offer them. We spend hours augmenting code for those what-if situations and ultimately end up spamming the metric search space with useless data points. Do not measure everything.

Back when memory was expensive, you had to be picky about what metrics to store. You had to focus on the most important ones for your service. As the cost of memory decreased, it became increasingly cheap to store increasingly more metrics—with a justification of providing value someday in the (far distant) future. For most of us, that future date never arrived.

The question then becomes, "What is worth measuring?" Focus on metrics that can build quality SLIs. First, let's describe the difference between metrics and SLIs. Metrics are raw numbers: how many items in a queue, how many days since the last failure, how many items in a shopping cart. SLIs are combinations of metrics that tell a story: if the queue keeps filling at the current rate, how much time is left before the system performance begins to degrade or completely falls over? Metrics provide evidence that the system simply works. SLIs provide evidence of how well the service works and on how long it will continue to work well. This is the customer experience story, and this is what you should focus on.

Customer experience impacts more than the paying customer, too. Every team member who uses your service or on-call staff member will also be a customer. As you work out what metrics to deliver, consider the 2 a.m. factor. When woken up in the middle of the night, will this metric help me or them get the service back up faster? Will this metric be useful for alerting? Will this metric accurately gauge the service's health? If the answer is no, reconsider your investment in that metric.

As the service matures, it is important to revisit your SLIs constantly. These metrics go stale as quickly as functions do. As you refactor your code, also refactor your metrics to verify that the SLIs are still appropriate. Take time for this work, because it will pay off tenfold in the long run, and make sure to signal to stakeholders the value of doing this, especially because the payoff isn't immediate. Be prepared to revisit your metrics monthly, if not more often. Reviewing often will lead to small tweaks rather than a drastic over-haul of stale SLIs.

This work can seem thankless, but it is vital; at many organizations, most metrics will never be looked at or read. A 2019 Twitter document (*https:// oreil.ly/wrUVI*) reported that less than 97% of metrics were ever read even once. In the case of Twitter, that's petabytes of metrics that will go unread. Navigating that metric search space is not easy without incredibly sophisticated tooling, of which many SRE and engineering teams will not have available.

Making the decision not to measure something can sometimes be daunting and may not seem like a debate worth having. But what should you do? Focus on your customers' needs and measure the SLIs that will improve their experience. This will mature your offering and prevent you from falling into the measure-everything trap. Your engineers will thank you for not having a noisy pager, too.

When SLOs Attack: Pathological SLOs and How to Fix Them

Narayan Desai

Google

SLOs are a wonderfully intuitive concept: a quantitative contract that describes expected service behavior. These are often used to build feedback loops that prioritize reliability, communicate expected behavior when taking on a new dependency, and synchronize priorities across teams when problems occur, among other use cases.

However, SLOs are built on an implicit model of service behavior, with a raft of simplifying assumptions that don't universally hold—assumptions such as the independence of requests, even distribution of errors, and the equality of all requests. These assumptions make SLO rules of thumb fall apart with real-world services. Understanding where and how these assumptions break down is critical: cases when SLOs inadvertently send us in the wrong direction.

Consider error budgets: a number or percentage of failures over a time interval. These errors could occur in a short period or at a low rate over a long time. They could be distributed across all users or focused on a few. Individual users could have low or 100% error rates. All these factors color how outages will be perceived and what kinds of effects they have on users.

Further, how best to deal with catastrophes? Many service providers try to incorporate bad days into SLO promises; however, some bad days are very, *very* bad days. This results in a compromise that serves in both fair weather and foul poorly. Neither is well described.

When things go really poorly, and multiple periods of error budget are consumed, what then? As appealing as the prospect of freezing a service for years may be, it rarely serves the best interests of either users or service providers.

Similarly, because error budgets often incorporate tail risks, they represent the P99+ bad experience. Hence, spending an error budget aggressively is a good way to deliver a consistently bad experience to customers.

Mismatches between SLOs and the average experience customers want can also lead to disagreements between service providers and their customers. Customers tend to expect the experience they received yesterday, even if that was a positive outlier on a service-wide basis, and changes to this behavior tend to cause their architectures to have issues.

At the end of the day, SLOs are about quantifying delivered service, setting appropriate expectations, and changing tactics when things aren't going well. All of these activities are crucial to deliver trustworthy services. So what can we do to fix SLOs?

1. Use different methods to describe discrete aspects of SLOs. Have steady-state error rate SLOs to measure transient error rates, but use bad-minute type SLOs to characterize major outages. Measure the frequency and severity of major outages and communicate them.

2. Measure and store per-customer SLI data to determine the experience individual customers are having and whether errors are evenly distributed.

3. Don't exercise error budgets unless your SLOs actually approximate the service you want to deliver to customers. This may or may not ever be the right thing to do for some services.

4. Embrace the ambiguity of many SLO measures; our services are rich, and a single aggregated measure of service goodness isn't possible. This approach leaves room for nuanced situational awareness and a variety of directions that can be used to improve user experience.

5. Set SLOs at actual customer-desired behavior in steady state, not incorporating tail risk.

With these guidelines, not only can we have SLOs that are less pathological, but we also get a series of metrics that we can use to improve our services in focused ways. With this, we can deliver reliable services with well-quantified behavior.

Holistic Approach to Product Reliability

Kristine Chen and
Bart Ponurkiewicz

Google

You've made it.

Through redundancy, you removed all single points of failure. The services are properly monitored and alerts are configured. Your recovery strategies are tested regularly to ensure that your on-call team can react on a moment's notice. You've carefully looked at your requests and announced achievable SLOs.

Job well done! Or is it? To ensure your product success, you have to take a holistic approach, end to end, from user interaction to the bytes on the disk. The typical front-end–back-end split isn't that simple anymore. There are layers and layers of abstractions. Your web service is a front end to your clients; it sends requests to your processing back ends, which are really just front ends for other services such as cache and storage servers. Turtles all the way down.

And we're only stacking more turtles on top: client-side applications. They come in various shapes and sizes, from progressive web applications up to apps running natively on smart devices. These apps have their back ends too: shared libraries, databases, and local storage. Reliable clients are now more important than ever, because more than 3.5 billion smart devices are currently used worldwide.

How do we start applying a holistic approach? Look first to dependency management and measuring the right things. We've all been here: a binary starts crashing and we're scrambling to find out what triggered it. Was it a release or a configuration push? If so, for which service? If you can quickly determine which part of the system changed, you can find the root cause faster.

This means knowing which back ends the client is talking to, which shared libraries are being used, and what dynamic configurations are being pushed. Ideally, your system will only interact with explicitly defined dependencies, so any new dependencies (read: possible failure points) are immediately visible during incident response, and any back-end service degradation can be attributed to specific user woes.

The most common metrics SREs look for are success and failure ratios of RPCs (remote procedure calls). But what if your client was crash looping on user devices? Your success ratio could actually go up, but that's cold comfort if your app is unusable.

Here's another example. For a service with one million QPM (queries per minute), a reasonable 99% SLO could exhaust its error budget through either 10,000 users getting a single error every minute or one determined user who retries 10,000 times and gets 10,000 errors every minute; the ratio is the same, but the experience is very different.

What should you measure then? Look at your users' ability to interact with the product: critical user interactions (e.g., opening a message and then deleting it). These interactions tell you whether your users can use your product. In addition, don't forget to slice your data by the count of users affected on different platforms and versions to make sure no group of devices is disproportionately affected by some failure mode for extended periods.

Times have changed; the internet is now more heterogeneous than ever, and most of the traffic doesn't come from PCs anymore. With a plethora of mobile operating systems on top of IoT (Internet of Things) devices, we can't pretend that the client side is not our responsibility.

Taking a holistic approach will help reduce the MTTR (mean time to repair). A few minutes of downtime might be overlooked by your users (just a glitch) but a few hours can lead to loss in user trust, bad press coverage, and potential loss of revenue. Extending emergency support to the client side will lead to even shorter response times and engender user trust when faced with an outage. Start from the user and work your way *out*. You'll thank yourself later.

In Search of the Lost Time

Ingrid Epure

Netlify

Who hasn't faced a significant outage caused by a problem you thought could wait six more months—whoops! How we wish we could have avoided this fire, and how nice it would have been to have had that time to prevent it. But we never do; time is the scarcest of resources in engineering.

We keep ending up in this place, and we know why. Infrastructure teams wear many hats: supporting product teams and running the existing systems, on call, developer workflows, and provisioning; the list can go on. With so few hours in a day and a finite number of resources, paying down tech debt and building automation and tooling get deprioritized in favor of feature work. After all, product is what sells; the company is trying to grow and stay alive, so most of the effort goes into acquiring new customers by building awesome solutions to their problems.

The deprioritization of this work robs us of the opportunity to be open to changes or figure out how greenfield work might fit in with the current work. In this world, wouldn't it seem more sensible to wait for a Holy Grail–type of project to solve a problem—to the detriment of small, continuous improvements?

The lack of space or time is why it takes some organizations so long to figure out things like CI/CD (continuous integration/continuous delivery). Instead of rolling it out bit by bit, they focus on the enormity of the concept and its associated risks. It's why we are still paged in the middle of the night for incidents that require reading a runbook and applying the same number of steps over and over again rather than investing in any sort of auto-remediation. All solutions feel huge, and time is limited, so what's the point in even trying!? We must carry on this old way and suffer.

The problem with not investing equally on both sides is that the cost of investment in reliability grows over time. The complexity added with new features adds more cognitive load on engineers, making it harder to work on reliability. The issues start to loom so large in our minds that we end up postponing until we can have more time, maybe in the distant future—until the inevitable outage.

Part of the solution is to prioritize working on something small toward the overall reliability goals every day, rather than working on it for a week and then moving on (and never returning). Organizing our days to fit shorter chores makes our brain feel more at ease and builds a habit. From a business standpoint, it also allows for more regular check-ins and continuous improvements.

How do we solidify this model? It starts with a commitment at the company level to create freedom for engineers to address consistently the reliability concerns they have on a project.

That freedom translates to time, which, depending on your engineering model, can be a percentage of the day, every day, or a week every X time (6 weeks to a quarter) dedicated entirely to tech debt. It's then followed by an agreement between engineering teams and infrastructure on the areas that could use the improvements most.

So next time you have 30 minutes, think about how you can get rid of something annoying. Thirty minutes a day adds up to 150 a week, 600 a month, and 7200 a year! Imagine what you could solve with that time!

Unexpected Lessons from Office Hours

Tamara Miner

Improbable Games

During a team retrospective at a prior job, one of the engineers suggested starting office hours so product teams could ask us questions about the tooling and services we provide them.

At the time, we struggled with low adoption of the tools we provided to product teams, tenuous relationships with their stakeholders or internal customers, and a lack of understanding of how to make existing platform tools (such as Prometheus) work the way product developers needed them to.

To be honest, I really didn't think office hours would solve the problem; we already had other communication channels, and we'd been unhappy with the lack of feedback from stakeholders. To track patterns and make changes to the process if needed, we set up internal monthly review sessions (and reduced the frequency to quarterly after we worked out the initial kinks). I expected to see patterns emerge, which might be easily solved with adding documentation, automating something, or creating a better process. After implementing Office Hours, we immediately noticed an improvement in communication between our team and other people in the company.

To encourage people to show up and say hi, it was suggested we bring in baked goods, so at minimum, I thought we would build some positive rapport with other teams through food, which might ease the tension between teams. To my surprise, even without baked goods, at least two people would show up at that hour each week. (Slack announcements increased that number significantly.)

Upon investigation, it turned out the Slack help channel was too intimidating because asking a question publicly felt like setting oneself up to be shamed if it was a dumb question. Not that that would actually happen, but the possibility was enough to deter folks. One unexpected pattern that became visible was that non-engineers started asking us questions, as did many more engineers who were either junior, just starting out with a particular technical area, or quite anxious—people who never asked us questions in our help channel! Instead, we created a welcoming space (with occasional banana bread) that created an informal safe place where people could come without fear of being a bother, publicly declaring what they don't know, or having stupid questions recorded in perpetuity.

Non-engineers don't want to interrupt or bother engineers by scheduling specific time to have whiteboard sessions for noncritical learning. Psychological safety is often discussed with regard to blameless postmortems, but it needs to be considered when developing an engagement model for SRE, period. Otherwise, it is likely that more will remain unsaid. We found certain questions only came up once we implemented Office Hours. For example, PMs (project managers) would ask about systems details or performance improvements. Office Hours created the perfect environment for stakeholders to feel safe asking these sorts of questions. After this, we saw engagement increase in our Slack help channels as well, because folks had built more of a rapport with the team and felt more confident that their concerns would be addressed.

Experiment with new vectors for cross-team communication and stakeholder management that take psychological safety and sociological patterns into account. I encourage you to find ways to bring humanity back into engineering conversations; make room for failure and asking dumb questions in a safe space. Remember that Slack requires some amount of professionalism, but Office Hours creates space for creativity and unstructured conversation, regardless of logical flaws. In our Office Hours, people stopped by just to say hi, which allowed for serendipitous conversation, innovation, and room to learn and grow.

Building Tools for Internal Customers that They Actually Want to Use

Vinessa Wan

New York Times

At *NYT*, no one is *required* to use my team's tools or follow our processes. Instead, if we want to win teams' hearts, we must build tools they want to use. To do so, we adopted a product management view that actively sought feedback in how teams perceived the value of our tools and processes.

Although quantitative metrics are vital, qualitative feedback can be over-looked in internal tooling. How do you find out about user—or, as you should start calling them, customer—satisfaction? You may not be able to collect the same scale of user-behavior data as external products can, but luckily, qualitative feedback from your colleagues is a great way to address that. Being able to reach out to someone in your company directory easily is actually a major advantage.

To start, identify desired outcomes. Are you trying to understand a problem space? Looking for feedback on a design? From there, we use a feedback process that includes a survey and follow-up interview process. A lot of advice is out there for how your team can gather feedback. Here's my take.

When building a survey, treat it like a product. Keep the user experience central in your survey design. The majority of questions should be multiple choice. Resist temptation to have multiple open questions such as, "Why did you score that way?" Before you send it out to a wide audience, test your survey to make sure it is easy to understand and complete.

Anonymous feedback, especially from your colleagues, tends to be the most honest. You can use other questions, such as job function or team, to ensure that you have a balanced response. For example, our first question gave respondents the option to leave their name if they were interested in talking with us. This took the pressure off respondents having to write detailed feedback and helped us build a base of people that were interested in sharing their experiences.

A survey is not a substitute for a conversation, however. Next, you should conduct user interviews. List your user types. Making sure that you have solid representation will help ensure that you are accounting for things you may not expect, as well as for blind spots.

Write out a certain number of open-ended questions, but watch out for leading questions. During the interview, refrain from interrupting the interviewee. Once they finish speaking, ask the interviewee to elaborate further on a point made. Each interview should have a facilitator and a scribe. Leverage your team as much as possible—our engineers volunteer to lead or scribe user interviews. Not only did this allow us to interview more folks but the team helped make improvements to the process.

Once you're done, synthesize and analyze the results with your team. Now, a caveat: take findings with a grain of salt. One interview does not mean you should upend your current plans. Share your results and plans. If you are trying to drive culture, it's important to demonstrate that you're not just listening but also have plans for change (or a reason you can't do something). It also helps to reference feedback-based improvements in future calls for feedback.

As a final piece of advice, remember that feedback loops should be regular and consistent. This isn't a one-and-done process, but one you continually iterate and build upon. And always question whether your processes are serving you.

It's About the Individuals and Interactions

Vinessa Wan

New York Times

> *Individuals and interactions over processes and tools.*
> —The Agile Manifesto

It's not that the tools or the processes don't matter, because they do, but often the biggest obstacle to creating a DevOps culture is ourselves and how we work with our teams.

As part of our data center migration effort in 2017, our leadership decided that teams would now be responsible for their own infrastructure. At the time, our centralized infrastructure team was largely viewed as a blocker for teams. Some of our larger application teams lacked skill sets and resourcing to migrate and build their applications in the cloud, so we started to help them. In some cases, this was us doing the work, actually sitting with their teams. Thus began our engagement model.

Early on we realized that for teams to be successful in the long term, we couldn't just do work. In particular, if SREs are constantly engaged with other teams, what about the SRE backlog? As a result, we adopted a shared-goals model. This helped us achieve a balance between reducing the automation backlog and engaging with other teams.

A shared goal was when we would collaborate with a team to build out features for their use cases or figure out a problem of which they would be an early adopter. The engagement was more about giving dedicated guidance or embedding with a team to help it on a project such as test automation.

After a few engagements, we built a process that allowed us to set up these partnerships for success. At the beginning of the engagement, we defined what success would look like and how we'd measure it. This goal would be on both teams' roadmaps.

We then set expectations of how the joint execution would work. For example, we wanted to make sure that our work would be a combination of guidance and building tooling that the team could use. We also spelled out who would have roles and responsibilities for things like ticket writing and how we'd keep updated on progress. For a more detailed explanation of how this model worked, I highly recommend reading my colleague Prashanth Sanagavarapu's essay (*https://oreil.ly/bkoWz*) in *The Site Reliability Workbook* (*https://oreil.ly/PneKu*) (O'Reilly, 2018). This may seem heavy-handed, but it eliminated confusion and saved time.

The engagement model also created some nonobvious benefits. By working with teams on tooling, we were sure it could work for them in the long term. It also gave us more insight into how different teams worked and used our tools.

These engagements were very effective, but it should be noted that they took a significant effort. These types of investments are very useful for teams in the initial stages of major efforts and can be reduced over time. We now limit our engagements to larger strategic efforts that involve multiple teams.

Remember, it's not about copying a process you read in the book or rolling out a specific tool. Reliability is a team sport. By focusing on our interactions, we helped build trust and empathy on both sides. Teams that partnered with us greatly appreciated what we did and were more willing to work with us in the future.

The Human Baseline in SRE

Effie Mouzeli

Wikimedia Foundation

There's no such thing as an SRE school. Site reliability engineering is a unique profession because the requirements to become an SRE are very broad, and the skills are not part of the curriculum of the average computer science degree. Organizations hire SREs with the assumption that they code well, have deep understanding of systems, know monitoring and alerting, can run any service, can debug production issues, can improve performance—and pull a rabbit out of their hat.

To have such range may seem superhuman, but instead requires a deep curiosity for how things work as well as the ability to learn from here and there. To be fair, it's unrealistic to expect everyone to know all that right from the get-go; we all come from different backgrounds and learn differently. Few of us can be deep experts among so many domains, so instead, we should rely on one another to keep leveling up each other's skills.

Leveling up should be a synthesis of mentoring and personal effort. Mentoring can have a profoundly positive effect on teams, improving the knowledge of both the mentor and mentee and creating stronger bonds. However, because mentoring requires time, energy, dedication, and, of course, good will, it is considered additional work. It usually doesn't count on performance reviews, is not recognized as delivering impact, and is not included in our team's planning. As a result, mentoring others becomes extracurricular, and leveling up ends up too often being a solo sport, left up to the person's discretion to achieve it.

It shouldn't be a solo sport, and one shouldn't feel alone in this. I believe that mentoring can be woven into day-to-day work. Here are some simple tactics to experiment with:

Take the long way home

Rather than assigning tasks to engineers who will perform them faster, consider having them assigned to engineers who have more to gain from it, with proper support/guidance from the team.

Mistakes and imperfections are okay

Within reason, it is okay to let people make mistakes and then let them fix them. Furthermore, it is also okay to accept an average solution that works and let the engineer improve it over time.

Pair systems engineering

This would be the systems equivalent of pair programming (*https:// oreil.ly/U6bti*), when two SREs perform a task *together* by, for instance, sharing the same screen.

Stepping back

During an incident, depending on severity, more senior engineers can step back and let the rest of the team investigate. Incident heroism produces results, but it may also overshadow the rest of the group and prevent the members from becoming confident enough to step up.

Integrating mentoring into a team's day-to-day work is a building block that can make it more inclusive and help it thrive.

When running services, we use baselines as indicators that our systems are performing well, but baselines are not limited to our production; they extend to the humans running it. The *human baseline* is a combination of soft skills and technical skills a team agrees a candidate should own to join it. Every so often we want to hire people who don't quite tick all the boxes, but at times, it might be better to invest in people we feel have prospects than to waste hours interviewing looking for unicorns. When we do so, we need to have the framework that will help new members get to the human baseline of the team and then above it.

Over time, skills can be improved with a little help from our team. Is anything more productive and efficient than a team that cares about each other?

Remotely Productive or Productively Remote

Avleen Vig

Facebook

As you switch from local or distributed to remote teams,[1] shifts in productivity can seem paradoxical. The assumption is that, away from the distractions of the office, people will skyrocket in productivity, whereas among remote teams, overall productivity can increase, but individual productivity might fluctuate or drop.

How does this happen? In every organization, critical work and less urgent work must be done. Productivity is the result of both of those types of work receiving attention. As individual productivity drops, people tend to refocus on one type of work or the other. If you're measuring success on the number of high-priority tasks or projects that hit their milestones, you may well see the overall impact of your teams go up.

Remote ICs (individual contributors) also have opportunities to be productive differently than they were before, and time-shifting work or breaking up their day is one good example of this. For example, ICs who are several time zones ahead of their colleagues can take advantage of quiet time in the morning to work on tasks with fewer interruptions.

A key element to keeping productivity high is communication and collaboration, and these are very human-centric. They require engaging with other people, listening, internalizing, and responding. The internet has considerable information about how to do video conferencing well or how over-communicating as a remote IC is important, but very few discuss the importance of social bonds.

Trust between members is an integral part of any successful team, and that trust is supported by strong relationships. In the pre-COVID-19 world, that happened when ICs sat, solved problems, and spent time together, learning

---

1 See You See Teams, I See Product, page 174, also by this contributor.

about each other. From my own experience, 1–2 weeks in the same location was enough time to let individuals be apart for up to 3 months and still maintain the same levels of trust and collaboration. After 3 months, those relationships would start to weaken and require more time together to refresh them.

In our new world, with more organizations turning to remote teams and less travel overall, this becomes significantly harder. We have to find ways to keep those relationships strong between teammates, on both a professional and personal level. Some suggestions include:

Video conferencing social hours
> Have people get together at the same time to talk about things other than work. Discuss special occasions, personal milestones, and events and make sure people are handling the increased isolation from their team well.

Multiplayer games
> Many are available, and some are free-to-play and widely accessible.

One-on-one conversations while having dinner
> These naturally provide a nonwork situation where people can talk about things other than work.

As a senior engineer on a large team, I spend a significant amount of time each week having 10–15-minute one-on-one catch-ups with other engineers. The key here is to find opportunities when we can engage each other in a social context.

The move to remote work may leave some individuals feeling less productive and getting less done than they are used to. It's important for us not to have knee-jerk reactions to this and realize that it's actually okay. Your organization should be constantly evaluating what more-important work it can be doing, making sure to focus on that. Some additional, less-critical work may fall by the wayside as a result. Accept and embrace this. If work that wasn't vital is being left behind while critical work is being completed as well or better, then things are trending in the right direction.

Of Margins and Individuals

Kurt Andersen

LinkedIn

Problem solving, beyond rote mechanical approaches, requires creativity, and creativity requires free space in which to take place. Understanding, empathy, and compassion all require the capacity to go beyond the constraints of immediate personal circumstances. That extra free space, that extra capacity is *margin*. Margin is the space between our load and our limits.

On a personal level, margin is critical to survival. One of the most fundamental aspects of life is breathing, and breathing only happens when the muscles of the diaphragm and rib cage make space—inflating the lungs and drawing air in. Constrictor snakes don't kill their prey by squashing them. They kill by depriving the victims of the ability to breathe by cinching tighter and tighter around the body until there is literally no room to breathe.

The pandemic and social disruptions of 2020 have highlighted the impact of environmental stress for nearly everyone. It is a powerful illustration of the concept of allostatic load (*https://oreil.ly/5DEOp*), a generalized stress response in the face of environmental uncertainty. As people have had to cope with increased environmental stressors, their capacity for other pursuits —their margin—has been degraded. As uncertainty persists longer or more intensely, people's mental and physical reserves are more deeply depleted.

To counter this environmental uncertainty, it is important to undertake renewing activities: breaks, changes of scenery, and exercise. Just like the rhythmic aspects of breathing, engagement and disengagement from work and attentional efforts is important (*https://oreil.ly/Zgrqr*) for mental and physical health. If you don't create and maintain personal margin, you will be on a path to burnout (*https://oreil.ly/HsQpe*).

On the flip side from the negatives of burnout, you can find the benefits of creativity that thrive in semi-constrained spaces. Allowing space for the unconscious mind to generate insights is why breaks and changes of environment can be so valuable. Many instances of dramatic insights have resulted from people taking their mind off a particular problem and finding insight from another source, such as Archimedes' "Eureka!" insight into how to measure the gold content of the king's crown.

Recent neuroscience research (*https://oreil.ly/3lD0Y*) has hypothesized that thinking intently about a particular problem can lead to a phenomenon similar to the Troxler effect, in which the focus of the fixation disappears. Taking a break can allow the brain to shift perspectives. Take time for yourself to think (*https://oreil.ly/ViH-H*). Your personal reliability depends on the space you make to ensure effective thinking.

In the practice of site reliability engineering, we have a key concept referred to as service level objectives—an explicit target for how a service responds, but potentially even more important is the extra part that is left over. Often referred to as the error budget, this leftover part is where or when the service does not meet the objective, but it's much more helpful to think about this as the learning budget.

We can extend this concept to ourselves. Just as incidents are unplanned investments in understanding your systems, the learning budget is where you get to explore new, creative approaches. The key to resilience is establishing and nurturing this adaptive capacity that lives in this space of the learning budget.

Lawrence Wilkinson, who works in the field of scenario planning, stated (as quoted by Tim O'Reilly[1]): "'robust'. . .means flexibility, adaptability, bias to learning, et al., [as well as] 'resilience.' . . . [O]ften hardest . . . is the need to sacrifice at least some efficiency to create slack, the elbowroom with which to respond. . .that is to say, the capacity to be effective."

It may be hard, but it's also critically important.

---

1 Tim O'Reilly (2020). "Welcome to the 21st Century: How to Plan for the Post-Covid Future" (*https://oreil.ly/L9k2H*).

The Importance of Margins in Systems

Kurt Andersen

LinkedIn

Margin is a tool for handling uncertainty and one of the multiple objectives that needs to be balanced when managing a technical or human system. In fields ranging from psychology to mechanical engineering to queueing theory and reliability engineering, the ability of a system to adapt (and in some cases, even perform at all) is critically dependent on the time and space buffers that are part of the system. Just as I've discussed the value of margins for individuals, margins are important for systems too.

Margins must be included in the design of functional systems to account for uncertainty and the additive effect of individual system tolerances. Computer networking is a great example of where the margin calculations are a standard part of the practice. Ensuring that every network link in the path has excess capacity beyond the expected bandwidth usage is a critical part of managing network performance. The older rule of thumb was to upgrade any links that were averaging 50% utilization; part of that was to account for lead times in the procurement process, but part of it was to handle unpredictable peaks in instantaneous traffic loads gracefully.

Newer guidelines, along with measures such as QOS (quality of service) prioritization, have allowed network engineers to push the average utiilization into the 70–80% range as long as they have good understanding of the traffic that transits their links. With less certainty, higher margins are required. If average utilization grows much beyond these levels, levels of latency and packet loss grow rapidly beyond acceptable levels.

The same fundamentals of queuing theory that lead to the need for margin in network engineering apply across many domains. An extensive body of research is related to scheduling operating rooms in hospitals, seeking to determine the optimal balance of utilization in the face of patient cancellations, uncertain procedure durations, and very expensive equipment and personnel resources. If you have encountered unacceptably long waits for a doctor's visit, it is probably because they were overscheduled, and the lack of margin caused latency in servicing your needs.

Like networks and operating rooms, teams also experience problems when they are overscheduled. This is the core principle in Dominica DeGrandis's *Making Work Visible*. Loads on teams are often neglected. Without a full picture of the workload for the team, they (or their management) can't properly assign task work while preserving the necessary margin for learning and handling unexpected changes.

Avery Pennarun[1] and Will Larson[2] has each developed simulations of how team productivity (in the sense of value delivered to the end user) fluctuates in the face of changing goals and too many tasks. These simulations highlight the importance of appropriate amounts of margin. In the face of greater uncertainty, more margin is required to keep the team producing effectively.

How much margin depends on the system. Without enough margin, a system will bind up when the slightest disruption causes widespread systemic failure because there is no adaptive capacity. With too much margin, a system fails to achieve maximal productivity because work is dissipated into the gaps within the system. As we work with complex, distributed, sociotechnical systems, we need to reevaluate our balance between constraints and degrees of freedom constantly to optimize the output of our teams and systems.

1 Avery Pennarun (2018). "The Math behind Project Scheduling, Bug Tracking, and Triage" (*https://oreil.ly/0sGHL*)
Avery Pennarun (2017). "SimSWE Part 1: Indecisiveness Simulator" (*https://oreil.ly/W89Jt*).
Avery Pennarun (2017)."SimSWE Part 2: The Perils of Multitasking" (*https://oreil.ly/aTbvD*).
2 Will Larson (2019). "Why Limiting Work-in-Progress Works" (*https://oreil.ly/Vbv8d*).

Fewer Spreadsheets, More Napkins

Jacob Bednarz

Napkin math is a process of performing calculations that provide an answer within a degree of magnitude of accuracy when you're unable (or don't need to) gather exact specifics, instead relying on using simplified assumptions. This is useful for confirming the viability of an option or narrowing the range of possibilities without spending hours or days on more complex calculations.

The kinds of estimation problems well suited for this are formally known as Fermi problems. A famous example estimates the number of piano tuners in a given city.

Assume that Chicago has a population of three million people, and each household contains on average two people. Say, one in 20 houses has a piano, and that it needs to be tuned only annually. Guess that piano tuners work eight hours per day, five days a week for 50 weeks per year (so, 250 days), and that each piano takes two hours to tune.

From here, we can quickly scratch out the following:

- Assume Chicago has a population of ~3,000,000
- Chicago has ~2 people per household
- (1,500,000 households) / (20 households with a piano) = 75,000 pianos in Chicago
- (8 hours per day) / (Tuning takes 2 hours) x (250 days per year) = 1000 pianos tuned per year
- (75,000 pianos in Chicago) / (1000 piano tunes a year) = 75 piano tuners in Chicago

Of course, there are most likely *not* 75 piano tuners in Chicago; however, we now also know there are probably not 1000 or even 10,000 piano tuners roaming the Windy City.

Let's apply this beyond piano tuners.

For instance, you want to know how long it would take to move data from a data center located on the US East Coast to another one located on the West Coast. Here, we can use a simplified representation:

- 60 ms (per gibibyte [GiB]) for the network trip
- 200 ms (per GiB) for the disk read (to send)
- 1 second (per GiB) for the disk write (to receive)

Using 1.5 s per GiB as the combined simplified time span, you can multiply that by the size of your data store and you have your answer! Now, this result won't be exact, but it gives an estimate within an order of magnitude of the actual result—more than enough to determine the viability of this approach.

You're starting to see the benefits of gathering a high-level calculated estimate because its application is broad and allows you to use seemingly impossible calculations to end up with an estimate within an order of magnitude of the actual answer.

The ability to move fast here is crucial because it means that you can make multiple calculations quickly to try out a range of options. This keeps the momentum going that is necessary for brainstorming to clip along without getting bogged down by granularity.

So feel free to start stocking up on napkins.

Sneaking in Your DevOps Deliciously

Vinessa Wan

New York Times

People are surprised when I talk about DevOps at the *New York Times*. I mean, we're over 100 years old. How did we do it? Driving culture change means you have to be viciously devoted to the cause. Taking every opportunity to champion the value, even if it means being sneaky about it. Any parent who snuck vegetables into their child's food knows what I'm talking about.

Maybe this seems deceptive. I mean, shouldn't we just be open that we're all going to be committed to reliability and just have our leadership know to prioritize it? Sure, in a perfect world, that's true, but driving culture change means you have to be not just passionate about the vision but also patient enough to know that folks will need training wheels for a while.

A DevOps culture means it's ingrained in everything we do. It's not just treating it as something special, but having it become a part of our DNA. This is why we shaped our election's readiness efforts—including that election needle everyone on the planet has heard about—to focus not just on a single night, but rather on how to lay groundwork for creating an operationally mature organization.

Instead of listing applications, we started with identifying key workflows, or key user experiences. Our users, or internal customers as we refer to them internally, are the Newsroom, Readers, and Business workers. A workflow example is, "Newsroom can publish an article to our website." Next, we would identify the systems required for each workflow. Systems that support a function can span multiple teams and even departments, but it shouldn't matter. Creating this view allowed us to focus on the overall experience of customers versus just a specific team. It also made sure everyone in the company was on the same page.

Each workflow and system in that workflow then was tiered to a level of criticality. We created expectations for each level of criticality. Combining this with a workflow view allowed us to view resiliency at both workflow and system levels. No longer would individual teams have to bear the burden alone.

We conducted architecture reviews with teams. This is a detailed evaluation of architecture to identify any at-risk areas, inventory runbooks, and discover how systems work together.

We led teams through an operational maturity model rubric that detailed practices such as service provisioning and decommissioning or capacity planning. This highlighted where teams can focus their energy and have the greatest impact on the reliability of their application.

We conducted performance tests on production periodically to measure how systems and teams handle increasing loads or various scenarios. Afterward, we held a learning review to walk through the timeline and identify how to improve.

If all of this doesn't sound particularly shiny, that's partly the intention. Like I said, we're the vegetables—but hey, vegetables done right are delicious. Sometimes vegetables are the star, and sometimes they are better as a stand-out backup singer.

I think not taking center stage in certain efforts and instead partnering and guiding those that are is a big factor in driving change through influence. My team is the stage crew of our site and apps. Still, I don't measure success in just one event—we have so much further to go and learn as an organization—but the aforementioned practices and processes allow us to focus beyond an event.

Our success is when you don't know we're there. In this very news-heavy period, our site continues to provide a reliable user experience that matches the quality of our journalism. Not bad for over 100 years old.

Effecting SRE Cultural Changes in Enterprises

Vanessa Yiu

Most well-established organizations have an ingrained set of practices, tools, and processes. Bringing on SRE means overcoming inertia and requiring a substantial investment of time to educate as well as continuous reinforcement of practices and behaviors.

Change is hard, especially in large organizations. Trying to change too much too quickly can result in confusion and lead to skepticism. We are creatures of habit—a sudden change of routines and operating outside of our comfort zone typically attracts initial doubt. Most cultural changes are also iterative and unlikely to be perfect from the get-go, so if people come across a bad experience or if something did not work out as intended the first time around, a negative perception can quickly propagate across the organization.

To avoid this, focus initially on the few most critical behaviors to adapt. In other words, find the key blockers to successful implementation of SRE at your workplace. If a shared responsibility model does not exist between developers and SRE, for instance, then perhaps start here, because that is foundational to getting SRE right.

After identifying your focus area, decide how best actually to *facilitate* the change in behavior. It is no good to want all services to have SLOs when the company has no such tooling, or to mandate blameless postmortems when forums where incidents are discussed do not exist. It is important to identify where the gaps are and then build a clear roadmap to lay the required foundations first. If you have effective tools and processes that are in line with the behaviors you would like engineers to adopt, this will eventually become routine and naturally lead to a change in thinking as well as in culture over time.

Cultural change is about people, not systems, so it cannot be approached with the same mindset as building software. A team of rock-star SREs does not guarantee success. In addition to hiring and training SREs, identify culture carriers in your organization who are adept at *empowering others and building trust*. Teach them the skills and help them spread awareness and knowledge across the organization. We are likelier to embrace change when observing and working with those who lead by example than by receiving missives from an ivory tower.

People at all levels need to participate, because it is unlikely to be just one person's responsibility or something that one person can get right when it comes to cultural shift. Top-down mandates are rarely successful in driving long-term behavioral changes across large organizations. Executives, however, do play a huge part in ensuring that the organization understands the change's importance and maintains focus, and regular top-down communication is key to achieving this.

Providing transparency and identifying the correct incentives are critical to the success of any large-scale change program. People need to see and believe the value for changes to stick. Be thoughtful about which results matter and which indicators reflect successful changes in behavior.

For example, if you want to encourage postmortems to curb repeating issues and mitigate risk, the true indicator of behavior change and success will be whether engineers are following through and closing out action items. Measure these and agree on the incentive structure to reward model behaviors, such as teams that use error budgets to drive decision making, or those who foster a blameless culture across the organization.

When everyone buys into and agrees to invest in a strategy, there can be the belief that getting this right will make the organization better, and everyone benefits as a result. Establishing an SRE mindset and its practices are foundational to the long-term, sustainable success of any SRE team.

To All the SREs I've Loved

Felix Glaser

Shopify

We've all come across an application pushed out of the door with questionable reliability. It makes our lives tougher when, inevitably, the application experiences its first outage and we are called in to help make the application more reliable. We aren't surprised by this but wish we would have been involved in the design and planning of the app and made reliability a first-class citizen. It's so avoidable—and it can wear us down.

I am not an SRE—well, not anymore. I returned to my first passion, security, drawn to strengthening the security of systems, protecting our users' data, and keeping the bad guys out. The change in perspective from switching teams led to an insight: security is to SRE what SRE is to product teams. We are here to support you to keep your systems secure, up and running, and ultimately reliable. In a way, we are *your* SRE team. Yet, you so often treat us the same way the single-minded product team treats you.

I've heard the complaints. You feel like we're slowing you down by being paranoid and always thinking of the worst-case scenario. What makes it worse is that we don't even have good data to convince you it's worthwhile. It's not like we can say, "You need to update this library or else the servers will be hacked."

Scaling up servers for the next DDoS (distributed denial of service) or flash sale is very tangible. See how many connections a single instance can handle, see how many people tried to connect the last time, and you just scale past that. As a security engineer, I have no way of pointing at that one CVE (Common Vulnerabilities and Exposures) piece that you need to fix or else. As long as you haven't been breached, there is no way to tell whether you're secure. There is no way to prove that a system is secure.

It's a thankless job; security teams aren't perceived as bringing the same value to a company as the SRE team, mostly because our work is nebulous. We have some great tools and techniques, including keeping operating systems, VMs (virtual machines), and containers updated; installing security patches; scanning the company's networks and IP (internet protocol) to detect all the software someone took online without consulting us; encouraging developers to update their dependencies; fuzzing their code before it goes out; and making sure permissions aren't over-granted. So we do the best we can, although if we do it well, no one will notice.

So what would make a production security engineer's life easier? Giving security the same room and attention you wish product teams would give SRE. Keeping us in the loop from the start. Communicating changes in infrastructure as early as possible. Involving us in the decision making. Not running an old operating system on a VM somewhere that you forgot about. Clicking Merge on that Dependabot PR (pull request) in a timely fashion. Trusting our recommendations. Ultimately, making us part of your organization by integrating us into your daily work and decision making. This has obvious benefits for you, because a hacked system might go down and cause a lot of downtime—and I would hardly call that reliable. So the next time we come to you with a seemingly paranoid recommendation, remember that we care deeply about keeping our customers safe and everything up and running. Don't let security become an afterthought!

And always remember: treat your security team the same way you wish that one product team treated you.

Complex: The Most Overloaded Word in Technology

Laura Nolan

Both software engineers and systems engineers use the word "complex" as a specific term of art. Software engineers use it in several ways, distinct from the systems meaning. Software engineers and systems engineers (SREs, production engineers, systems administrators, DevOps practitioners, etc.) are overlapping groups of people who work together. We all need to understand which meaning is in use at any given time so we can communicate clearly.

Complexity has been the enemy of the software engineer for decades now. Fred Brooks' classic essay, "No Silver Bullet,"[1] divided software's complexity into two parts: essential complexity and accidental complexity. Essential complexity is related solely to specifying the problem and how it should be solved. Accidental complexity is related to the details of implementation. The overwhelming majority of the work of technology operation is about accidental complexity.

However, this doesn't tell us what software engineers mean by complexity. Fundamentally, complexity is that which makes software difficult to understand fully and to reason about correctly. Moseley and Marks' paper, "Out of the Tar Pit" (*https://oreil.ly/0-iuA*), discusses several sources of complexity. The biggest, and hardest to deal with, is state. State influences the flow of control of a program, but the number of potential states that a piece of software can be in increases exponentially with the number of variables.

Other major sources of complexity are sheer code volume and the fact that programs, unlike complex physical structures, cannot be visually inspected.

---

1 Brooks, F. P. "No Silver Bullet." *Essence and Accident in Software Engineering.* Proc. IFIP Tenth World Computing Conference, (1986), 1069–1076.

Mental models of the program must be constructed from the source code. This can of course be easier or harder, depending on how the code is structured.

Systems engineers tend to have a completely different idea of complexity, stemming from systems theory. Complex systems have particular characteristics: multiple interacting parts, system state (i.e., a memory of some kind), and feedback loops. They display emergent phenomena, have nonlinear relationships (small changes in one part can lead to large deviations in overall system behavior), and tend to be prone to cascading failures or vicious cycles. Complex system behavior cannot be predicted reliably.

All computing systems are complex systems. Even if a system is running on a single physical machine, you are still dealing with the interactions of multiple pieces of software, all of which are likely complex systems in their own right, running on complex hardware. Each running program may have multiple threads of control, state, interactions with the operating system and other programs—even if not explicitly, then through shared resources.

This systems theory definition of complexity is the one often used by systems administrators, SREs, and DevOps practitioners. Software engineers, on the other hand, mainly think in terms of code structure, interactions between modules, and interdependencies in their code bases. Software engineers' primary concern is the difficulty of making correct changes without introducing errors. Systems engineers' primary concern is stability of the deployed software in production.

This is why, when you ask a software engineer to promote simplicity as part of their job description, they look for opportunities to separate concerns and reduce coupling in their code base to refactor to well-known design patterns, create better-defined interactions between modules, and remove unused code. When you ask systems engineers to do the same thing, they often look for ways to control extremes of the system's behavior (using load shedding and circuit breakers, for instance) or to make elements of the system more uniform.

The two kinds of complexity that we discuss here are quite different, but they do also have one major thing in common: both software complexity and systems complexity make the task of understanding and predicting behavior impossible.

PART IV

Ten to Hundred

The Best Advice I Can Give to Teams

Nicole Forsgren

GitHub

If I had to say one thing, it would be this: *integrate your teams.*

That's it. That's the advice. Work together. Talk more.

If there's one thing we've learned about developing and delivering software over the past decade (or more), it's that more communication and fewer silos is key. It really is all about information flow. It should come as no surprise that this applies to SRE teams, too. Carving off another special team simply creates a new silo, and their work and influence can't reach those who need it most. By separating the SRE team from the development teams they support—sometimes by creating a Center of Excellence—you end up causing more problems than you solve. Separating SRE from dev teams leads to a few problems, including:

Elitism

I get it; it feels good to be part of the special club, but by isolating expertise, you simply create a bottleneck and limit the ability for others to get work done. This can lead to everyone coming to you for everything in a case of learned helplessness, or coming to you for nothing because the process is too hard. Neither of these is good because they remove you from important, high-priority work.

Knowledge constraints

When one central group owns and hoards all the knowledge, it becomes harder to share, mentoring is more difficult, and best practices become more difficult to scale.

Separation from the work

A big chasm between SREs and the teams they support can feel like someone dictating how things should be with a translation layer missing in between. If you never work with the development teams, it can be hard to get a real feel for their work. They can also have a hard time grokking the reliability and scalability issues that keep bouncing back to them; their environments just fundamentally behave differently.

Sponsorship

Office politics aren't always fun, but this is an important piece to remember: SRE is typically executive-driven and -sponsored, making the CoE structure a risky move. If your sponsor leaves the company or no longer sees the value in what you do, you may be left without strong connections to the rest of the company, and your function may be eliminated. That's not good for you, your teams, or your users.

What are the best ways to integrate? Of course, find a way to do this that works best for your organization. One solution can be embedding SREs into dev teams, with regular meeting cadences to share work, best practices, and patterns that are cropping up around the business. (By fostering this loose structure sometimes known as a Community of Practice, you're getting the best of both worlds: a shared community without the costs of silos.) However, there aren't always enough SREs to embed in every dev team. (Who are we kidding? This is the dream.) Some organizations solve this by having their SREs do rotations through dev teams and sometimes by having developers do rotations into SRE.

By working together and being partners in the software delivery process, SREs can help organizations of any size focus on the users' perspective, prioritize the right work, and adopt systematic approaches to improving reliability and availability. At the heart of it all is communicating and collaborating.

Create Your Supporting Artifacts

Daria Barteneva and
Eva Parish

Microsoft
Squarespace

Don't underestimate the power of documentation to support you and your organization during SLO implementation. Your goal is to break down SLO creation into three phases: *define the SLO, collect SLIs,* and, later, *use the SLO.* Here is a list of the documentation we recommend at this stage:

One-page strategy document

This will be the most important document in the crawl phase. What are you trying to accomplish? Why? How? This will be the very first document you share with people when they ask, "What is this effort all about?" Make it short enough for anyone to read in less than 10 minutes. It's critical that you get this document right. Use this book as a resource to help you articulate *why* your organization needs SLOs: what it will get out of creating SLOs, and how SLOs will improve service reliability for your users and help your engineering teams. Make sure you review this document with your leadership and have its sign-off and total support for the strategy you plan to communicate across your organization.

Two pages defining SLOs (high level)

Next, you'll need a more detailed (but still brief) document that explains what an SLO is, gives examples of good SLOs, and tells the reader how they can get started. You don't want to scare your readers by asking them to read an entire book about SLOs just to understand what an SLO *is.* Make it easy for engineers to get an idea of how to implement SLO-based approaches and try to build their interest.

FAQ

Collect a list of the questions you expect people to ask as they begin their own SLO journeys, and compile them into an FAQ document. To start with, you might include questions like:

- What if my user is another service? Do I still need to care about SLOs?
- What if my service's dependencies don't have SLOs?
- How many SLOs should a service have? How many SLIs?

Defining SLOs for your service, step by step

You'll need a document that explains, step by step, how someone in your organization can define an SLO (the first phase of the SLO creation process). Don't talk about instrumentation and metrics collection here; focus on the high-level process. You might want to share an SLO definition template that teams can use.

Instrumenting your service to collect SLIs

As a follow-on to the previous document, this document will give step-by-step guidance, with examples, on how to instrument a service to collect SLIs (phase two). You can be very specific here and look at the monitoring platform your organization uses to give examples of SLI instrumentation for different types of services. For example, how would you collect latency data and translate your metrics into SLIs, using percentiles? How would you instrument a pipeline service to collect SLIs? Give as many examples as you can and provide ready-to-use code snippets, making it easy for engineers to move forward with the monitoring instrumentation step of the journey.

Use case

If you've already implemented SLOs for any of your services (or for the example service you developed while doing research), write up the details in a use case document to give your SLO early adopters a concrete example of how this is done.

Don't forget to define where all your artifacts will live—for example, a wiki paired with a code repository—and make sure they're discoverable and easy to navigate to. The biggest mistakes we see across engineering organizations are not taking the time to create well-structured and discoverable technical documentation, and not demanding that documentation undergo the same quality review process as code.

Adapted from the book *Implementing Service Level Objectives: A Practical Guide to SLIs, SLOs, and Error Budgets* (*https://oreil.ly/kAVJt*) (O'Reilly).

The Order of Operations for Getting SLO Buy-In

David K. Rensin

David K. Rensin

Google

As the person driving your team, organization, or company toward the adoption of SLIs, SLOs, and error budgets, you will have to do a fair amount of convincing. For some people, the basic arguments for SLOs will run counter to the goals they have set for themselves and their teams. Others will want to prioritize feature velocity ahead of reliability work, and still others will doubt that the company is mature enough or good enough really to adopt these principles and techniques.

It's important to realize now that the benefits of adopting an SLO-based approach will not be self-evident to everyone and that you will have to do a fair amount of patient explanation. Let's build a game plan to get everyone on board. Like most things in engineering, the order of operation is important.

Based on experience, here's my suggestion for the order in getting buy-in:

1. *Engineering and operations*

    Your first step is to get both the engineering and operations teams on board with SLOs. This should be reasonably straightforward because SLIs, SLOs, and error budgets offer real benefits to each group. Their mutual agreement to the principles of SLOs is essential to getting other teams on board. Note that I said *principles*. The implementation details (error budget policies, SLO targets, etc.) will be negotiated later.

2. *Product*

    Your next stop is probably your product managers (or whoever writes the product requirements documents, or PRDs). The key argument you are making to them is that this approach will give them better feature velocity over time. They will want to know that engineering and operations are on board, which is why they're in step 2.

3. *Leadership*

Once the engineering, operations, and product teams have bought in, it's time to talk to your senior leadership. The benefits of this change (greater release velocity, early insights into the user experience, a better work environment, etc.) are obvious, but they will want to know that the big three are in agreement.

4. *Legal*

Your next stop is the lawyers. You aren't likely to meet much resistance here if you've completed steps 1–3. They will be concerned (rightly so) about what this change will mean to the public SLAs (answer: if they aren't already fielding lots of SLA violations, then these changes will have almost zero effect and may present an opportunity to adopt more competitive SLAs; if they're fielding more than they'd like, that number will go down).

5. *QA*

This is your last stop. This is the group that will be most concerned about what these changes mean for them. The important part of this conversation is to keep the team focused on the skills they bring rather than the organization they joined. Nobody is going to lose their job—far from it. You're not really there to *convince* the QA team. You're there to inform them (gently) that the company is moving to SLOs and that leadership, engineering, product, and operations all agree this is the right thing to do.

You will need to talk to other groups—sales, marketing, customer support, and so on—but they are consumers of this decision, not the implementers.

Adapted from the book *Implementing Service Level Objectives: A Practical Guide to SLIs, SLOs, and Error Budgets* (*https://oreil.ly/kAVJt*) (O'Reilly).

Heroes Are Necessary, but Hero Culture Is Not

Lei Lopez

Formerly Shopify

Building healthy, sustainable cultures requires understanding the difference between heroes and hero culture. Heroes are made in crises, when people perform extraordinary tasks to save the day, but that doesn't mean you should encourage the catastrophes to force people to become heroes—that's what hero culture does.

Think about when your SREs receive widespread praise. In my experience, it's usually in response to a nighttime incident when someone has sacrificed sleep to save the day. Events like this garner praise from coworkers inside and outside of engineering. Yes, we must recognize incident responders performing heroic acts, but it becomes dangerous when it veers into glorifying this work.

True heroes spring to action when they are needed but wouldn't wish anyone else, including themselves, into those awful situations. SREs in a hero culture push an organization toward an operations-versus-development mindset, the very mindset site reliability engineering is meant to move *away* from. Developers neglect sharing responsibility for their services with SREs. Why worry about shipping the more reliable option when there's an SRE on call to save the day?

Hero culture therefore discourages preventive work. If work is only recognized when resolving an emergency, people are encouraged to focus on work that presents itself as an emergency! This is when dumpster fire–driven development kicks in: when something desperately needs to be fixed but isn't urgent, and buy-in from above only comes in once it's a dumpster fire (i.e., has become an incident).

The motivation for heroes is internal because people want to do good work during extraordinary times. In a hero culture, motivation comes externally because people are only rewarded for being thrown into situations in which they must perform extraordinary work to keep things running. We need to recognize and reward preventive work.

When a problem can only be solved by a handful of people, and those people feel that positive attention only happens when they're the key to saving the day, not only (ironically) do they become potential points of failure, but the environment translates into a heavy on-call burden. As they reliably answer the call to fix things, expectations build that they'll fix things every time, and the organization doesn't work to avoid the issue. Constant firefighting is a sure path to burnout.

Shifting back to heroes from hero culture requires finding new ways to recognize work. One reason this is so difficult is that it's hard to quantify when something *doesn't* happen. We have to make predictions.

I think about the Stoic practice of negative visualization, when you imagine a version of your life with worse events, like losing your job, to realize gratitude for your current situation. The premortem, a time to imagine what would cause a project to fail, is a celebrated tool in SRE. Let's use it *after* the project has shipped, to celebrate the things that *didn't* happen and the people behind the nonevent.

Similarly, we must remind developers of what they can do to prevent or reduce the harm from these situations. This should also be a tripwire for leads to invest resources in technical debt. This is the perfect time to engage everyone in a team effort to make things better for their *shared* responsibilities.

Hero culture is easy to fall into, but an SRE mindset can be applied to combat this. We can recognize that heroes do their best work as part of a team, and true heroes don't need a hero culture to do good.

On-Call Rotations that People Want to Join

Miles Bryant,
Chris Evans,
and Suhail Patel

Monzo

At Monzo, on call is so popular that our rotations have a waitlist. Unfortunately, that's not the case for most organizations. Our industry has resigned itself to the idea that on call is painful and a necessary evil. Thousands of developers and SREs put themselves through misery and burnout because it's part of the job. But must it be that way?

We don't think so. Our efforts show that a well-designed, human-centric on-call process pays off by having enthusiastic, motivated, and effective engineers on our rotation. How did we get here? By putting people first.

On callers are human. This is what makes on call so powerful; when safety systems, resilient architecture, and automated remediation stop working, no machine even comes close to matching the capability of a human to react and adapt to a novel failure in a complex system. Unlike machines, humans cannot withstand 24/7 uptime or sustained 100% CPU usage. Burnout sucks; it sucks for the people around them, it sucks for the company losing a smart and capable engineer, but it *really* sucks for the person. Effective on call is also humane on call.

First, we incentivize people. Many on-callers aren't paid at all (*https://oreil.ly/ nYSBq*); it is only fair for companies to provide compensation for the added burden, responsibility, stress, and disruption to normal life that the pager imposes. People are also motivated by the opportunity to progress technically and learn much more about the systems they work on. We encourage and reward this by including on-call behaviors in our developmental and career-progression framework (*https://oreil.ly/XkEMr*).

Second, we address the pain of being on call. Reducing the frequency of being paged is an obvious starter; although we'll never practically achieve 100% reliability (or there wouldn't be a need for on call at all!), we can reduce the number of noisy alerts and failures through automation and careful monitoring design. We treat every page as an exceptional circumstance; if no action is required, we tweak thresholds or even delete alerts.

Third, a good on-call experience starts from the moment someone joins the rotation. A common experience is to be thrown in the deep end and expected to handle things alone. Trial by fire is not a prerequisite for being good on call; at Monzo, every on-caller shadows a more experienced engineer for a few months so they can practice incident response and gain context with lower expectations with a knowledgeable and confident hand to guide them.

Last, strong on-call culture doesn't happen overnight; instead, it comes from constant effort and frequent iterations. We have a graveyard of bright ideas we tried that didn't quite make the cut; at one point, the on-call schedule was manually handcrafted in a spreadsheet, like a jigsaw puzzle.

The best source for ideas to improve on call is the on-callers themselves. We hold frequent retrospectives and reflect on ways we can make on call better. Sometimes it's nice to have a forum just to vent, but our most useful improvements and ideas often have come from collaborative reflection. Giving people agency and a chance to better things is a powerful way to empower on-callers and improve their well-being.

You can, and should, improve on call. Our systems are becoming more complex yet critical, and increasingly we rely on humans to step in when automation fails. Building happy, healthy on-call rotations is a superpower and one that you, too, can gain by taking the time and effort to incentivize people, reduce the pain points, provide mentorship, and iterate rapidly.

Study of Human Factors and Team Culture to Improve Pager Fatigue

Daria Barteneva

Microsoft

Noisy pagers can lead to pager fatigue, but noisiness is a subjective idea; every team will have its own threshold of alerts for a noisy pager. There's an assumption that more must mean worse, which led me to wonder: does the number of pages correlate to on-call satisfaction? To find out, I looked at an organization of ~200 engineers divided into teams of between 10 and 20 people, with a mix of experienced and junior engineers. Engineers rated their on-call satisfaction and provided verbose feedback about their experience. The results surprised me. A higher number of pages didn't correlate with on-call satisfaction.

I looked at the teams that scored high in satisfaction and had a high number of pages, and shadowed them to learn more about their engineering practices. It turns out that human factors and team culture played substantive and important roles in empowering engineers to feel more positive about their on-call experience.

Pager fatigue is not about the volume of pages; one can have two pages but no sense of agency to change the situation, whereas another could have 20 pages and thrive on driving durable improvements in the system. I found that satisfied teams had engineers with autonomy and were empowered to drive the change in the system where it mattered most. In addition, discussing ideas and celebrating achievements were consistent practices. This resulted in a positive feedback loop, accountability, and collaboration opportunities and helped to avoid duplication of work. Let's review some engineering practices from teams with higher on-call satisfaction:

- *Technical literacy and hands-on experience* were two of the big contributors to on-call satisfaction. Successful teams had established effective onboarding processes and invested in training and keeping their documentation up to date.

- *Good communication and collaboration* had a force multiplier effect on team efficiency. Successful teams had multiple weekly meetings that were attended by 90% of team members together with the manager, who actively contributed to the meeting but didn't dominate the discussion. This helped build the *bottom-up culture* with *top-down support*. Engineers reviewed incident trends, systemic problems, documentation improvements, automation, and so on. Any follow-ups resulting from those meetings resulted in logging a work item and identifying an owner. Dedicated meetings did detailed *incident retrospectives*, following the Five Whys process. *Blameless culture* was a critical component of all discussions and focused on platform and processes rather than on the individual. Engineers felt safe sharing their opinions.

- To build a *culture of accountability and ownership*, but also to celebrate achievements, teams had recurrent Engineering Reviews and Demo meetings, with a predefined agenda or an open mic style. Both kinds of meetings, structured and unstructured, established different team collaboration dynamics. Any blockers and changes in priority were communicated and discussed in a timely way.

- Teams established an effective *feedback loop to ensure that everyone's voice was heard*, and on-call satisfaction was measured over time. On-call engineers would fill in surveys as soon as their on call was over, including verbose feedback about short-term and midterm improvement recommendations. Survey results were regularly reviewed and acted on.

- Finally, highly satisfied teams demonstrated high levels of *empathy*, looking proactively at opportunities to support each other.

The volume of pages was not always a good measure of on-call experience. This number was less important than the approach to it. A culture of trust, ownership, accountability, effective communication, and collaboration was critical to building a successful team. It established the foundation to improve processes and technology that in return drove better on-call experience and service reliability.

Optimize for MTTBTB (Mean Time to Back to Bed)

Spike Lindsey

Shopify

It's the middle of the night. The loud, distinctive sound from your paging app of choice rudely yanks you from sleep, shortly followed by a call, then a message for good measure: you wouldn't want to miss a page!

Doing *anything* after being suddenly woken up is not ideal—dazed, cortisol levels spiking, maybe even some adrenaline—let alone debugging complex systems under pressure. However, this is the reality of being on call for many, because few organizations can invest in follow-the-sun rotations across all their teams, yet operate systems that need 24/7 availability.

Over time, with enough frequency, out-of-hours pages become a source of stress and eventual burnout. The human cost is not trivial. Part of the solution is fixing the causes of pages, but we have to acknowledge that some pages will still happen. Knowing this, how can we best support on-callers and reduce the mental and physical toll of holding a pager?

First, ask, "Will this make sense if you've just been woken up?" Even the most experienced, expert on-callers are not operating at full capacity upon interrupted sleep. We must actively reduce the cognitive load of incident response—whether through checklists, runbooks, scripts and tooling, or dashboards—thinking carefully about whether the information provided has enough context to be effective but not so much it causes overload.

Take into account users coming into a situation with very little initial context. Breaking a wall of text (or comments) into single-sentence, simple bullet points may seem like overkill, but it is so much easier to process when still sleep-addled. Clearly flagging any steps that are tricky, dangerous, or irreversible also goes a long way. If escalation is needed, provide a clear escalation path with contact details and escalation thresholds.

Second, ask, "Does this get you back to bed faster (and keep you there)?" This draws focus toward mitigation and exit criteria. At night, a complete and comprehensive fix should never be the goal; instead, the focus should be on mitigating enough that the whole team can look at it with more rested eyes the next day.

Setting explicit expectations about when something is considered mitigated (but not necessarily fixed) and giving people permission to end an incident as soon as they think it's safe to do so can help reduce a tendency for on-callers to stay up and babysit the system by staring at dashboards. Remind on-callers that there's no point staying up—if it breaks again, they'll be paged again anyway.

Tying these together is the notion of practice during daylight hours; the worst time to do something for the first time is in the middle of the night, during an incident. We do on-callers (and ourselves) a disservice by not checking things over before an emergency situation, and removing the rough edges where possible. In the same way that we regularly test fire extinguishers and smoke alarms, we should also test our tools and processes.

Being paged at night sucks, but doesn't look like it will go away any time soon, especially given the scale and complexity of the systems we can build at speed with small teams. Getting people to think about the human side can help them empathize as well as draw on their own experiences. As an added bonus: if it works well at 3 a.m. with someone half asleep, it'll probably work even better with someone fully awake.

Mitigating and Preventing Cascading Failures

Rita Lu

Google

Picture a toppling stack of dominoes, each one knocking over the next until every domino has fallen. Cascading failures can happen when a theoretically loosely coupled system actually has tight connections that we're not aware of. In production systems, when an overloaded region fails, its traffic shifts to healthy neighboring regions, which become overloaded and fail in turn. Unchecked, cascading failures can progress quickly, leading to a global outage of the system within minutes. This category of failures has been the culprit of large, public outages of services such as GCP (Google Cloud Platform)—and even electrical power grids.

There are multiple ways to trigger a cascading failure. A sudden spike of traffic overloads a component in a system. A seemingly innocuous code or configuration change that produces performance regressions, thus reducing capacity, can be a cause despite no increase in overall traffic.

When a cascading failure happens, many overload symptoms present simultaneously, making it difficult to debug and mitigate in time before it spreads to a global outage. The number one goal should be to break the chain. Front-line mitigations may vary, but here are some of the core ones that are applicable to most situations.

For an initial regional overload caused by a change, identifying and rolling back this change allows the query cost to return to normal. Capping already affected regions to reduce load can help them recover and prevent them from becoming completely unavailable.

Front-line mitigation procedures should be well-documented, regularly tested, and fast to deploy. Even when an expert team of engineers has mitigations ready on hand, it can be difficult to mitigate a cascading failure completely, without any serious impact on users.

A more effective strategy toward a resilient system is prevention through improving system design. Performance and regression testing in the canary phase of a release can catch performance regressions, such as memory leaks, before a global rollout might cause a capacity shortage.

Better load throttling can make regions more resistant to overload by rejecting or degrading responses when a task has reached its capacity. Load test a region to determine the ideal utilization to target at the load-balancer level so that individual tasks do not become overloaded. Configure a sensible task-level, load-balancing algorithm (such as weighted round robin) to keep tasks as equally loaded as possible.

Stronger isolation between regions can ensure that regional failures do not spread globally. In this setup, redundancy in each region must be maintained separately, since neighboring regions can no longer compensate for each other's capacity. This approach can be costly but offers the strongest guarantee of isolation.

Beyond the system is the toll on humans. Imagine, Friday afternoon, everyone's ready to pack up for the week. The on-call engineer's pager rings. She sighs and takes out her laptop to take a look. Very quickly, the entire team is scrambling to apply mitigations as error rates skyrocket. Rollbacks and caps are being deployed the quick and unsafe way while a pager storm signaling global overload goes off. Tickets from customer support are flooding in. Soon, the director and VP are on the phone, demanding to know time to mitigate.

This is unfortunately a typical situation when a cascading failure occurs. Even when multiple mitigations are applied, it may take dozens of minutes to stop the overload entirely. In addition to the system at risk are the people under stress trying to handle the situation. Even when the system recovers, the impact on people can remain. This is why prevention is better than cure; the only way to avoid customer-impacting outages is to build a system resilient to cascading failures.

On-Call Health: The Metric You Could Be Measuring

Caitie McCaffrey

Microsoft

A sad trombone noise emanated from my phone one Saturday afternoon. The services I was on call for requested attention, yet again. It was the end of my first week on call for a new team, and I had already been paged at least 50 times. I was bleary-eyed and anxious. As I acknowledged the alert I had a strong urge to throw my phone into an adjacent brick wall. Instead I took a deep breath and scrolled through the alert details while firing up my laptop yet again.

We define SLIs, SLOs, and SLAs for service health. We measure availability and reliability, run postmortems that focus on customer impact, and implement health checks for services to detect failures quickly. As an industry, we're quick to know whether our services are healthy, but we overlook a crucial component of running a successful service: whether the people on call are as healthy.

Are they sleeping through the night? How often are they being paged outside of business hours? Does the work of being on call fit within a reasonable workweek? Fortunately, we can use several of the tools and best practices for monitoring a service's health to monitor this other critical component.

Metrics to measure

To understand service health, we define SLIs; for measuring on-call health, we need similar metrics. Note the number of alerts per week, the severity of alerts when fired per week, the number of outside-of-business hours alerts. Think about the resolution of alerts. Was the alert noise? Or was it actionable?

Monitor metrics and remediate issues

On-call health metrics should be reviewed regularly. I recommend weekly, as part of a regular on-call review or hand-off process. Just as we would with service health metrics, look at week-over-week trends of on-call health metrics to detect emerging patterns. Use this weekly review to ask questions such as: Was this an uncharacteristically busy week? Or has the number of alerts per week been steadily increasing? Are they actionable or mostly noise? This time should also be used to schedule follow-up items. If the alerts are noise, they should be tuned or eliminated. If the alerts are mostly actionable, are there recurring tasks that can be automated?

On-call postmortems

It's important to get regular qualitative feedback on the on-call process as well. Just as we use postmortems to surface qualitative feedback and learnings on service health, we need to do the same for on-call health.

I recommend running regular anonymous on-call health retrospectives. I like using a mixture of quantitative and qualitative questions. Ask questions with numerical scores. For example, on a scale of 1 to 5, how disruptive is being on call to your work–life balance? Include free-form questions such as: What's the worst part of on call? What takes up the majority of your time when on call?

Once all the feedback has been gathered, it should be analyzed and a set of follow-up action items aggregated and added to the team's backlog. Just as with postmortems and other retrospectives, for this to be an effective tool, it's important for the action items to be scheduled and completed in a timely manner; otherwise, this is a waste of time and will frustrate the on-call engineers.

This may seem disconnected from the technical side, but remember: if your service is meeting its SLOs and SLAs, but your on call is unhealthy, your service won't stay healthy for long. Unhealthy on calls will lead to fatigue, burnout, and attrition. Long term, these will have a negative impact on service health and the business objectives it supports.

Helping Leaders Prioritize On-Call Health

Caitie McCaffrey

Microsoft

You understand that on-call health is a critical feature of running a successful service. You are an individual contributor or dev lead who has done your homework. You have read the articles, seen the talks, followed hashtags like #oncallselfie, and always send #hugops to your friends working at other companies during major outages. Or perhaps you have learned the benefit of on-call health the hard way, by being on a team with a horrific on-call experience. There's just one problem: your leadership team does not seem to value on-call health as much as you do. So how do you help leadership understand that on-call health is just as important as any feature?

Bring Quantitative Data

Help your leadership understand the impact of on call on your team by bringing hard data. Charts and graphs, with trends over time, are great and can really help convey a lot of information quickly. Often, on-call health is talked about in qualitative terms; these are valid and important, but it can be difficult for a lead, who has less day-to-day context, to assess the impact on call has on a team. However, there are quantitative metrics that can be measured as well. (See On-Call Health: The Metric You Could Be Measuring, page 152.)

It is much easier for leaders to understand the impact of indisputable metrics, such as that the on-caller was paged every night this week during after-work hours, than qualitative feedback such as that on call is disruptive to work–life balance. Helping leaders quantify the impact should help make your case.

Link SLAs to On-Call Health

Availability metrics and on-call health metrics are inextricably entangled. All attempts to separate them are subterfuge. Bad on calls will result in missed SLAs, which will lead to unhappy customers. By consistently linking SLAs and on-call health metrics, you'll help your leadership understand this symbiosis. How do you do this?

Include on-call health metrics in availability reports
> You are likely already tracking and reporting SLA attainment to your leadership. Start including on-call health metrics.

Include on-call health in OKRs
> If your team uses planning tools such as OKRs, set goals for your SLAs and for on-call health metrics. I'd recommend having a high-level objective around service availability. The OKRs can measure things such as SLAs, success rate, and latency, and an on-call health metric such as number of pages per week.

Treat On-Call Health like a Feature

During your planning process, account for on-call time. Assume that while on call, a dev is actively dealing with incidents or is using that time to improve the on-call experience if it's a quiet week.

This can be as simple as creating tasks for the on-call dev to ensure that this work is being accounted for in stand-ups and sprint planning. If you do a larger quarterly or per-semester planning process, include on call as a feature and allocate time to it. Typically, this should be one dev per week for the planning cycle. Highlight this investment to leadership during the planning process.

By incorporating on-call work in your team's planning process, you will help your leadership see this as work that can be planned and budgeted for rather than as an interruption that the team must just absorb to keep the schedule.

Measure Attrition

Finally, help your leaders understand that sustained bad on calls will lead to attrition. However, attrition is a lagging indicator of bad on-call health, and using this metric should be viewed as a last resort, because at this point, the situation is dire.

The SRE as a Diplomat

Johnny Boursiquot

Salesforce/Heroku

Although there are common through-lines, no two organizations implement the practices of site reliability engineering in the same manner—a fact that is, unfortunately, seldom recognized, much less acknowledged, when rolling out an SRE function for the first time, especially in organizations where teams have traditionally operated with complete autonomy and independence from one another.

For organizations where teams have complete ownership of a service from its development all the way through to its ongoing operational needs, it's common and necessary for team-specific practices to develop. This total ownership model works well to move business objectives forward in the early part of a system's life cycle, but it eventually and insidiously morphs to become unaddressed technical debt when maturing teams need to adopt shared reliability practices and tooling.

The drive for maturation that is supported by engineering leaders will, undoubtedly, include the attempt to inculcate standardization as a result of having identified heterogeneity of processes and tooling among teams to be a barrier to the incremental march toward operational excellence as promised by SRE adoption. Although beneficial on the surface, these changes are hard for teams to absorb due to the impact on what they do and how they do it. As long as feature demands keep coming, operational improvements will often take a back seat. Bridging this gap between the intent of leadership and the practical implications within teams requires change agents in the form of SREs who can be embedded in these teams.

The teams that see themselves as self-sufficient are not always incentivized to work with a traditional and external SRE function requiring changes in how they operate—even when those changes would markedly improve things. Regardless of the reasons, building bridges across these teams requires us first to establish trust. One way to facilitate this trust-building is to take the nontraditional approach of embedding SREs directly in those teams, analogous to establishing an embassy on foreign soil to improve relations with other countries.

These SREs act as diplomats, working at the crossroads of the needs of stakeholders seeking successful adoption of SRE practices within sizeable engineering organizations. They tackle problems by gathering the concerns, constraints, and conditions across teams to surface a path forward where all teams benefit in the long term. They balance the immediate operational needs of their host teams with the long-term objectives for operational excellence across the whole engineering organization. They are specialists who must carefully initiate and facilitate strategic agreements across teams and with engineering leadership on behalf of their host teams.

I call these diplomats "forward-deployed SREs," or fdSREs. Implementing SRE requires close collaboration among engineers, operators, and leadership, facilitated through interpersonal skill and diplomacy. The fdSRE is at the crossroads of the needs of stakeholders seeking successful adoption of SRE practices in sizeable engineering organizations.

As the practice of SRE continues to be adopted throughout our industry, engineering teams soon realize that the published best practices do not always fit neatly into their organization for a number of reasons. What SRE looks like for your teams will require some creativity and a willingness to break the prescriptive mold put forth in off-the-shelf models. When trust and alliance-building are what you need to move SRE adoption forward within your organization, give diplomacy a chance.

To learn more about the qualities of an fdSRE, see my essay, The Forward-Deployed SRE, page 158.

(The learnings shared in this piece come not only from lived experience but also from conversations with the following colleagues and industry peers, whom I'd like to thank here: Sarah Sherbondy, Paul Lathrop, Will Barnette, Steve Conklin, Kimberly Lowe-Williams, and Christian Funkhouser.)

The Forward-Deployed SRE

Johnny Boursiquot

Salesforce/Heroku

SRE teams are often independent of any other and operate with their own objectives and mandates within the broader engineering organization. However, the embedded model is another approach that isn't often talked about, but that can be effective when seeking SRE adoption or investing in ongoing operational excellence. In The SRE as a Diplomat, page 156, I discussed the need for the fdSRE (forward-deployed SRE) as a manifestation of the embedded model. Here, we discuss the attributes that make a great fdSRE.

As with SRE, the fdSRE is a competent but operationally minded software engineer. As they engineer software, they think about how it will run in production, how it will behave under load, what configuration will look like, what security and/or compliance will look like, how it will regain a consistent state when restarted, and how it will be observed.

The fdSRE takes on more ownership. As an embedded engineer in another team, they are concerned about the health of their host team but also about the broader mission of the SRE organization with which they have a dotted-line reporting relationship. In the total ownership model, where teams own the whole stack, the impetus to solve a higher-order problem that affects everyone can be lacking. The fdSRE must learn to build relationships and engender trust to identify solvable problems they can take back upstream. As fdSREs share their common pains with each other, they can then build the most impactful solutions and act as conduits throughout the organization.

The fdSRE is empathetic. As with any person joining a new team, it can take time for the fdSRE and the host team to gel. The team may not know whether the fdSRE is aligned with them, but over time, as they work on problems together, that trust gap has a chance to close. The fdSRE must understand this and give the host team members room and time to acclimate to their presence.

The fdSRE is a catalyst for change but knows not everybody is ready for it. They inspire the desire for change and give people space, time, and the data to want to be part of the solution. To that end, they meet teams and individuals where they are on the journey to increased operational maturity.

The fdSRE is a teacher and mentor. Chances are that nobody on the host team will have the same level of operational expertise as the fdSRE. Having an SRE on the team who can impart knowledge is extremely valuable and can be exciting for host team members to help them develop that operational mindset. Inclusive of the fdSRE's duties is the education and growth of other engineers.

The fdSRE is a diplomat. There is a human side to the role that is invaluable. They understand that every team ultimately wants to have a positive impact on the organization and that sometimes trade-offs and compromises must be reached through tactful negotiations, not mandates. This can take the form of providing data, asking about pain points, and understanding and working the channels that help decisions be made.

If you adopt the fdSRE approach, be prepared for a deliberate effort to be put toward collaboration between engineers across teams and with engineering leadership to drive all parties toward the safe creation and maintenance of scalable and reliable software systems, and know that the effort is worthwhile.

(The learnings shared in this piece are also informed by conversations with the following colleagues and industry peers whom I'd like to thank here: Sarah Sherbondy, Paul Lathrop, Will Barnette, Steve Conklin, Kimberly Lowe-Williams, and Christian Funkhouser.)

Test Your Disaster Plan

Tanya Reilly

Squarespace

Systems fail. That's fine. Site reliability is a whole discipline that specializes in anticipating and mitigating failure. We build systems that are observable, introspectable, and recoverable that limit the blast radius of an outage. We design for failure.

Failure planning often includes fallback plans, alternate pathways through our code, and systems or processes that we'll use when our regular mechanisms fail. A client may retry a failed request, for example, hoping it hits a healthier replica next time. A leader-elected system may move leadership away from an unresponsive server. Fallback plans sometimes involve humans; every time we page an on-caller or take some action in response to an outage, we're executing a fallback plan.

Our regular pathways are constantly in use. We know they work, and we notice when they fail. Many of our fallback plans are also well-traveled, running so frequently that we'll find out if they have problems. What about the less-traveled paths? If we only use them during emergencies, we might not find out they don't work until we really need them.

An extreme illustration of this problem is an industry classic: the gently rotting disaster recovery site. A team anticipates a massive failure of their primary site and builds a replica of their system in another region or another data center. They configure their deployment pipelines to push to both regions, set up data replication, and call it good—until disaster strikes and the failover region is needed for the first time. Now at 3 a.m., with all hands on deck, the team finds the hard-coded DNS names that point to the old region, the forgotten passwords, the commented-out replication policy, and the fixes too temporary to copy to the DR (disaster recovery) site—fixes that are, of course, now vital infrastructure.

We need to discover these problems while we can still fix them. That means testing our fallback plans. Some of these tests are simulations. Many organizations run game days, when they practice responding to typical disaster scenarios, sometimes reproducing them with test data. Teams can test their own response with local wheel-of-misfortune exercises, role-playing a possible outage in detail so that the team has to go find real logs, graphs, configs, even the phone numbers of their colleagues—anything they might need in a real incident.

Role-playing for disasters helps us uncover the parts of our plan that don't work or that we don't quite understand. They build muscle memory and reduce panic too. Think about how building fire drills have trained us to walk calmly to the meeting area without freaking out.

Simulated disasters are helpful, but it's even better if we can make the fallback plan part of our normal operations. The first time you fail over to a DR site, intentionally bypass your cache, or firewall-off one replica of a service to test its redundancy. It'll be pretty scary. You may break something. But the best time to break it is while you're watching it and can quickly roll back. It will get a little easier every time.

As with all things reliability, the priority of testing the fallback plan should be proportional to how important it is to the business. If the worst outcome of failure is that some teams will need to do extra work, maybe that's an acceptable risk. If the fallback plan is the only thing standing between you and the end of your business, take it very seriously.

A disaster plan can only keep you safe if it works. Identify your fallback plans and try them out. Make sure that they're ready when you need them.

Why Training Matters to an SRE Practice and SRE Matters to Your Training Program

Jennifer Petoff

Google

When it comes to site reliability engineering, there is a lot to learn. Whether you are aspiring to become an SRE or ramping up on a new service, you may feel like you are drinking from a fire hose of information. You need to learn about the ins and outs of complex production systems, incident management best practices, and more.

For adult learners, and especially for people new to a team, imparting technical knowledge is not the top training-related consideration. Instead, building confidence and fighting impostor syndrome are most important. Beyond instilling confidence, training is also about driving or perpetuating a desired organizational culture. Training is an investment in your organization and people.

So where should you begin? I have one acronym for you: ASSBAT, which stands for *a student should be able to*. ASSBATs are learning objectives that focus on behaviors you want to drive and observe. Understand, the $foo service is a bad ASSBAT. Better ASSBATS might include:

- Use $tool to identify how much memory a job is using.
- Interpret a graph in $monitoring_tool to identify the health of $foo service.
- Move traffic away from a cluster by using $drain_tool in five minutes.

By using these types of ASSBATs, you can observe and measure how training is applied day to day. Start with ASSBATs, and you've equipped yourself with the beginnings of a great training strategy rather than relying on hope.

Now let's get meta. This essay is about training site reliability engineers. Did you know that the foundational principles of SRE can be applied to the training program itself? Let's revisit the Service Reliability Hierarchy outlined in the original SRE Book (*https://oreil.ly/3emUN*). The hierarchy covers the elements that go into making a service reliable, from most foundational to most advanced. The elements of the Service Reliability Hierarchy can be adapted to the training context (see here (*https://oreil.ly/aMduh*), p. 84).

First, *monitor* the performance of your training program in the form of attendance tracking and survey feedback. Define SLOs (service level objectives) for the training program and communicate them.

Address issues that surface through monitoring. If a survey response comes in for which certain questions are scored negatively by a student, this calls for investigation and follow-up to understand what went wrong. Was it a curriculum issue, a logistics issue, or an instructor issue?

Write *postmortems* when things go wrong to learn blamelessly from failure. Writing a postmortem when an issue significantly affects the student experience allows the training team to define action items that drive real improvements to the program.

Always *test* new content and programs with pilot sessions. For the test teaching session (pilot), make it clear to the students that you are testing new material, and leave time at the end of the session for feedback.

Scale operations by looking for opportunities to vanquish toil through automation to make the most of limited human resources. Only then can the program be fully actualized and achieve the full potential of the *curriculum design* and the *program* itself.

Too often, companies allow a sink-or-swim strategy for training. Not only is it ineffective, but as I've shown, effective SRE training is within your reach. Thoughtful training ensures that you are setting your people up for success while walking the talk by applying SRE principles to the program itself to drive continuous improvement.

The Power of Uniformity

Chris Evans,
Suhail Patel,
and Miles Bryant

Monzo

Every organization wants to move fast, so it's important to understand the things that can slow it down. In SRE, those often derive from one or more among friction in making changes or understanding how to, complexity of the operational domain, and freedom of choice. At Monzo, uniformity is the key to keeping us moving; uniformity has led to consistency, consistency has led to focus, and focus has allowed us to build the fastest growing bank the UK has ever seen.

Like all startups, we began with a small group of engineers responsible for the entirety of the company's technology, from the low-level physical infrastructure to the microservices serving customer requests. With a small team and a blank canvas, we needed to focus our effort where it was needed most —on building a bank. The layering of standard approaches simply meant we became increasingly efficient at solving actual customer problems. Rather than starting from zero on each iteration, we could focus our efforts on the 10% that really made a difference.

This isn't about stamping out freedom of choice or imposing unnecessary constraints on innovation, but instead about providing a set of defaults that work so well that it's hard to make a case for doing anything else. When an engineer can create a service with handlers, metrics, logging, and signal handling and debugging endpoints *and* ship it to production in minutes, it's hard to justify the cost of starting from scratch. With a well-trodden path and a shared understanding that the benefits of following that path extend beyond the local maxima of any individual or team, people become naturally more judicious about where they spend their innovation tokens.

Maybe you're reading this, thinking, "This can't work at my organization." Uniformity shouldn't be seen as an absolute. What is uniform to one company could be proliferation in another. A long-established organization with a diverse portfolio of systems and applications can still define approaches that converge on uniformity. It's easy to look at the landscape and assume you are beyond recovery, but try drawing a boundary around what you have today, and a smaller one defining where you'll take your next steps.

If you have six programming languages in circulation, and a subset is serving the needs of most engineers, uniformity could mean standardizing on that subset for all future development. Given clear principles and constraints around choice, any company can move toward a more uniform, simpler-to-operate system.

With everyone working from a common framework, uniformity is a force multiplier. The efforts of any individual on any shared component have a positive impact on every other engineer in the organization. If we fix a bug in a library, everyone benefits. If the fix requires a large number of services to be redeployed, and they're all deployed in the same way, we easily do that too.

Operational activities become easier in a uniform environment too. Services become measured by their differences in business logic, and when every engineer understands the common components and communication patterns of all services, it's easier for them to support both their own services and those they interact with directly.

Systems are growing increasingly complex; consistency in common components means reduced cognitive load, faster execution, and a focus on what matters most to your business. For us, what was born out of necessity and unspoken convention evolved into a well-defined set of principles and practices (*https://oreil.ly/OKVnU*) that engineers now live and breathe, with one common platform, one programming language, one framework for all 1600 microservices, one deployment process, and one way to monitor everything.

Bytes per User Value

Arshia Mufti

Stripe

I remember a time during which we were growing steadily as a business, but the systems teams that supported our product stayed stagnant and over-loaded, and its arguments for increasing head count fell sort of flat. Our leaders didn't understand that our teams needed more people. As far as *they* were concerned; business was growing, and the areas that deserved investment were not systems teams but product teams that needed to build new features, sales teams that needed to onboard new users, field engineering teams that had to help developers integrate with our API. There was a serious lack in our ability of our systems teams to speak the language of our users and stakeholders. We didn't know how to stitch together stories that involved both end users and the foundational systems that they depended on.

So instead of starting with ourselves, we started with those end users. We pulled data on user growth and asked ourselves how we could demonstrate that investment in our infrastructure is inherently correlated with the growth of our business.

From there, we were able to tell a story of how growth in a user's business brought with it an increase in API volume, which in turn put a proportional burden on our infrastructure. Instead of showing that we were scaling up servers more frequently than we did before, we quantified how much of our increased scale was demanded by the fastest-growing users of Stripe and used this argument to leverage an investment in our reliability.

We were also able to demonstrate to others what we already knew: that systems teams absorb a disproportionate amount of the manual toil needed to keep our businesses functioning. We are paged more often, our user asks have grown, and our pager-interrupted hours are longer. Most important, we showed that these interruptions were, on average, a *direct* result of the unexpected growth of some of our users, and that addressing them would be in the best interest of our business's health.

It isn't enough to say, "We don't have enough people, so give us more." It also isn't enough to say, "We processed more bytes per transaction this quarter, so give us more money." The argument that everyone needs more money, more people, more servers, and more resources within an organization tends to be a zero-sum game. Ultimately, what helped us make a convincing argument in favor of investment in our teams was proving to our leadership that a change in the forces they care most about percolate down to our systems teams.

More broadly, I've been thinking about why this seems to be such a challenge for the infrastructure industry. Product teams have well-exercised processes for wholly understanding their users. For them, it's not just about giving the users what they want; it's about understanding what they *are like*: their use cases, their worries, and their constraints. In systems engineering, we have yet to establish similar user-serving paradigms. We don't know how to hire for it, we don't know how to teach it, and we don't quite know how to understand its value. Our fallibility lies in that we optimize first and only for the immediate consumers of the services we operate, and are quick to categorize any other problems they have as out of our scope. This is somewhat organic; we naturally tend to be more degrees of separation away from end users than product teams are, but it is nevertheless worth a course correction. We need to teach ourselves to break free from the technicalities of our systems and understand the people that our systems ultimately affect.

Make Your Engineering Blog a Priority

Anita Clarke

Shopify

Every engineering manager I know wants to hire the best talent possible, and yet they can neglect one of the strongest tools in their kit: a great engineering blog.

Talented developers are hidden everywhere across the globe. Some may be familiar with your company's work, whereas others haven't discovered it yet. An engineering blog raises a company's profile to an audience that is magnitudes larger than the average conference attendance, especially if your post picks up steam on, say, Hacker News.

Candidates make decisions about your company's offer based on the quality of the engineering blog. I've heard it enough times from senior SREs and leadership to understand this is a major thing. Hell, it's the first thing my Director said to me when I joined their team. Culture is one of the most important factors to a candidate, and to recruit successfully, it should be a mandatory part of your storytelling efforts.

An active, highly regarded engineering blog makes you more attractive to candidates. Yes, it's a lot like dating in a way; SREs want to do that Google investigation on you first, and a great blog makes an effective first impression.

So don't make it fluff. The blog is actually a great place to share information about what you're working on, and fill it with as much substance as you can. Peers experiencing the same issues can use your solutions to overcome them, or if you're sharing an issue not solved yet, peers can reach out after seeing the post. For SREs using open-source tools, these connections and discussions are crucial. We all help each other when collaborating on open-source solutions. These posts kick-start the vital conversations by raising awareness.

Storytelling gives life to inert, vague job titles, adding clarity and excitement instead of head scratches, figuring out what this job title means compared to industry standards. They see the tech stack and its usage and in-depth analysis of the choices and trade-offs teams make along the way in their projects. In short, an engineering blog gives candidates insight into working for your company that isn't possible during the interview process.

Now, this needs to be intentional. If you hope that high-quality blog posts will randomly spring out of your engineers by themselves, when they already have enough work to do, you'll be disappointed. It's stronger when there's a dedicated individual or team whose sole focus is to help make these compelling stories powerful, professional, and promotable.

Blog posts are collaborative learning efforts. Writing requires research regardless of years of experience. You see a ballet dancer's graceful and fluid motions, but you don't see the bloody toes that go with it; that's writing. However, know that the effort will be worth it. Through the writing and editing process, everyone learns more about the topic through this feedback loop by sharing, discussing, and reevaluating ideas. An engineering blog is not only great for recruiting; it's a key component of a strong learning organization.

Don't Let Anyone Run Code in Your Context

John Looney

Microsoft

My team runs a machine-installer service. Submit a request for a new OS, and your machine is netbooted into a RAM disk, which sets up the disk and downloads an OS. Customers wanted to be able to tweak all disk settings; choosing a filesystem type wasn't enough.SREs love smart hacks; they enable extra functionality without a lot of work, but some classes of hacks are anti-patterns, and the short-term gain is nothing compared to the long-term pain. We thought we were clever by letting customers provide a shell script to be run before the OS was installed. This script might create partitions, RAID arrays, and filesystems. As long as a root filesystem was mounted after the script terminated, their machine got an OS.

Fast forward several years. There are hundreds of shell scripts, some no longer used. Others are forked copies of scripts from machine owners long gone, and bugs found in one script weren't backported to its original. Due to bugs in customer scripts, 2% of attempts to provision machines failed! This impacted our service metrics and gave customers the impression that we provided poor service. They weren't wrong.

There were many causes for the failures. Some drives don't support all hdparm commands. Assumptions were made about device size. Some broken SSDs silently drop writes, and when you read back the partition table, it will be zeros. Drive and RAID setups can fail in thousands of ways. Some scripts were 1800 lines long—without unit tests.

We had accidentally built a system dependent on hundreds of our users being able to write defensive shell scripts in a world of unreliable, changing hardware. Our unfounded optimism was rewarded with a constant stream of hard-to-debug issues. Our smart hack turned out not to be very clever.

The only answer was to *take our users' code out of our team's context*. So we built a system that used validated user-provided JSON, describing what the disk layout *should* look like. We promised customers that we would make the disks look as they wished and take responsibility if *our code* caused problems. It was a pain in the ass to reverse-engineer the 350 shell scripts, work out their intent, ensure that our disk-layout tool supported the dozens of use cases on hundreds of platforms, and then migrate everyone to the new configurations, but once it was done, our provisioning reliability went from 98% to 99.8% overnight.

In tens of thousands of servers a week, 99.8% is still a lot of failures, and investigations uncovered another smart hack that was causing intermittent problems. When customers gave us machines, we would first ensure that the machines were drained of traffic and data. To do this, we ran a drain script. Guess who wrote these—our customers, and of course, if their scripts crashed or hung, it looked like we were taking a long time to reinstall the machine.

Thankfully, we know how to fix this! *Take our users' code out of our team's context.* Have our customers drain machines before they ask us to reinstall them. Refuse to accept undrained machines. It may seem like a minor semantic difference, but from an SLA perspective, we cannot offer a meaningful SLA if we are beholden to code we don't own.

Never let your customers feed you code; insist on validated configuration! Never give an SLA on a service that contains code from other teams! Never offer an SLA on a service that includes unreliable dependencies! You cannot abdicate your responsibility to understand deeply what your customers do with your service. Defend your service and your team's reputation for good customer service!

Trading Places: SRE and Product

Shubheksha Jalan

Historically, there's been a tension between SRE teams and product and feature teams akin to the wall between ops and dev teams. The former want to optimize for reliability first and foremost, whereas the latter want to ship, which leads to change—which leads to things breaking. We don't need to live with this oppositional relationship. If we can build empathy between product and SRE teams, it will not only lead to a healthier relationship, it will be a stronger win–win outcome for everyone.

How does this happen? It's important for engineers on both teams to be in each other's shoes to understand and make the right trade-offs. When product engineers don't operate with a reliability mindset, they shift an unfair burden onto SREs that can lead to unpleasantness and, in the worst case, burnout. When SREs don't adopt a product-engineer perspective, they might not understand the pressure from executives and stakeholders, and both teams miss the opportunity to broaden their knowledge.

The ideal scenario here would be for each feature team to be responsible for running its own service rather than for the SREs to be paged in the middle of the night. However, this isn't always possible. On call is hard. It can be disruptive and taxing even when done well. If it lacks empathy or care, it can have disastrous consequences. Engineers can't and shouldn't be forced to be on call. Some folks do not want to be woken up in the night and have pretty good reasons for that opinion, such as having a chronic illness or caring responsibilities. This can't work if people are unhappy with the on call. We need to create feedback loops to have a healthy on-call culture.

This is where we want to get to, although I understand that teams can't start there from the get-go. However, we can have a somewhat hybrid solution here by letting engineers rotate on the other team periodically for a duration of, let's say, two quarters. (That duration, of course, depends on your organization, and you'll want to find the balance that works best for your teams.)

This will lead to better understanding and collaboration between the feature and SRE teams in the future, when members of each are aware of the issues the other team faces and the kind of trade-offs they have to make on a daily basis.

This also helps you expand your skills as an engineer, because SRE work can vary greatly from day-to-day feature work. It can open your eyes to a brand-new domain that you've been working adjacent to but haven't gotten a chance to explore. If SREs know how product teams function, they can use that insight to make the platform more reliable. Product engineers tend to be the ones who talk to customers, and SREs can be shielded by it, so SREs can learn about customer demands directly. SRE teams responsible for platforms see product engineers as their customers. When SREs rotate with product engineers, they are in a way talking to customers.

Engineers should have *some* idea of how, where, and why their code is being run and thus ship the best version of the software possible. This gives them a chance to do exactly that, leading them to become much more holistic engineers overall.

You See Teams, I See Product

Avleen Vig

Facebook

In 1967, Melvin Conway coined Conway's Law, as follows:

> Any organization that designs a system (defined broadly) will produce a design whose structure is a copy of the organization's communication structure.

Over time, organizations have learned the value of not only having strong communication and collaboration between teams, but also of structuring it in specific ways. This becomes part of the team culture, and it instructs ICs on how to behave both as individuals and in groups.

Conway's Law should be applied in reverse by organizations. Find the way you want your product to behave and create an organization whose communication structure emulates it. If your product has a high social factor, you probably want to encourage a lot of communication between teams. If your product is used in highly regulated industries, you may want to create a more process-driven, hierarchical organization.

The place you land on the spectrum between microservices and monolithic applications depends on how well the components in the system, and individuals on your teams, are able to communicate. If the interfaces are well designed, robust and resilient, and don't change very often, you may lean toward microservices. If your team spends a lot more time trying to figure out the latest correct way to talk to each other and they have a high degree of chatter, you may lean toward monolith. There is no wrong answer, but keep in mind that these are both sides of the same coin.

The challenges since the emergence of COVID-19 in late 2019 have forced many of us to ramp up on different ways of collaborating and working. Companies with local, distributed, and remote teams have different challenges.

Let's first define the differences between local, distributed, and remote teams.

Local teams

The vast majority of ICs and their managers are located in the same office.

Distributed teams

The team consists of 2 or more geographically diverse local teams. For example, you may have 4 engineers and the manager in New York and 5 in London.

Remote teams

The majority of ICs, and possibly the manager, are in different locations.

My main interest here is to discuss remote teams, because they present more challenges in defining and creating cultures, and many organizations have yet to take the first steps in adapting their existing cultures to being remote-friendly. Look at the ways your teams and groups are structured today and find ways to emulate the most important links for when employees move to being remote.

The structural challenges remote ICs face, especially early on, center on communications and autonomy. ICs need to act with greater autonomy due to their relative isolation, make more decisions themselves, and communicate those to their peers. In a software product, you could imagine multiple independent processes doing their work and communicating the results over a shared protocol.

Creating and managing remote teams still needs the same design and process as creating local teams, but now you also have to think more deliberately about the culture you want to promote. It's far easier to get it wrong when most of the people on the team are far apart, but be patient with the process, because the investment is worthwhile.

The Performance Emergency Fund

Dawn Parzych

LaunchDarkly

SREs rely on concepts such as error budgets to manage changes across the organization, whether that means determining whether a release can move forward or identifying where to make improvements. Error budgets are related to availability, but of course, you need to know not just whether you're available but also the quality of that availability.

If you're not thinking about the quality, then you're only getting part of the picture—but how do we define quality? I'd argue that one of the most important ways is through performance. How do you feel when it takes what seems like forever to load? Or performance on your smartphone is slower than on your laptop?

Everybody in an organization should care about performance. If a site loads too slowly or inconsistently, you run the risk of lost customers and lost sales. Nobody wants that.

Numerous studies have shown that faster-loading pages result in higher revenue, increased user engagement, and a decreased bounce rate. Slow-loading pages can also be an early indicator of a problem. Catching a problem due to slowness is better than waiting for a failure.

Just as you can create an error budget, you can do the same for performance. A performance budget is a clearly defined limit on performance metrics used to guide design and development. You can have multiple budgets for different metrics. Here are some that I think are especially valuable:

- Total page weight
- Maximum file size
- Response time thresholds
- Number of HTTP requests

Similar to bringing together different parts of an organization to consider SLOs (and, by extension, error budgets), you can do the same for performance as well and gain invaluable insights from the range of points of view. Find out who in your organization cares about the end-user experience and work with them to devise a performance budget if you don't already have one. The creation of a performance budget should include stakeholders from design, marketing, operations, and engineering—it is truly a collaborative effort. The creation and maintenance should not fall to a single team.

Performance budgets reflect ongoing and changing business goals while allowing for risk and experimentation. Flexibility notwithstanding, the team must agree not to exceed the currently defined budget. If all teams agree on the performance budget from the start, each feature and design decision will be checked against the guidelines. Any decisions that might impact performance should be checked against the budget. Performance budgets provide another layer of accountability when site changes are proposed.

We must always think from the perspective of the customer. Does the customer care whether the site is up or down? Yes. Does the customer care whether the site loads without errors? Yes. Does the customer care whether the site loads quickly? Yes. If the customer cares, you should too.

If the site is up but users are abandoning the site because it took too long to load, that's not good for business. In the end, the work we do doesn't matter if it doesn't align with business goals and objectives.

Important but Not Urgent: Roadmaps for SREs

Laura Nolan

Former American President Dwight D. Eisenhower organized his work according to importance and urgency. Important and urgent tasks were done immediately, and unimportant tasks were delegated or ignored. The most challenging quadrant of Eisenhower's matrix was the intersection of important and nonurgent—things that made a difference but also were easiest to defer indefinitely. Eisenhower's approach to this kind of work? Plan.

Eisenhower's dilemma applies to SRE teams too. Have you ever worked with a problem system that constantly generated toil or downtime but was never redesigned? Ever noticed a team that disagreed over long-term technical direction, in which only one person drove strategy or, worst of all, in which nobody seemed to have a plan that extended past the end of the current quarter? These are the organizational smells of a team requiring a roadmap.

A roadmap is a high-level description of strategic work that a team wants to accomplish in the next couple of years. All SRE teams ought to have a roadmap because it helps teams think beyond the immediate and instead reflect on what work is important. We are engineering teams with operational responsibilities, which lead to urgent, reactive work: putting out fires or acting on requests from other teams. It's normal (and fine) for some of our work to deal with immediate needs, but teams that operate only on the urgent side of the Eisenhower matrix are limited in what they can achieve. A roadmap is the best way to avoid that trap.

Many problems we face cannot be solved incrementally, because they require engineering investment over multiple quarters. Teams in perpetual firefighting mode can get stuck in a local maximum, using short-term fixes to keep things running but never making larger changes to eliminate underlying issues.

For example, a team might spend years on a better recovery-and-restart process for a single-homed service. Instead, it could invest in re-architecting that system to run as a multi-homed service that can survive the loss of a data center. The second approach eliminates a source of stressful toil, risk of data loss, and downtime for good, but that project could take a year to complete. It's the sort of project that's only possible using a roadmap.

Roadmaps set out what a team should do in the long term, why those objectives are important, and the relative priorities of those goals. A roadmap isn't a laundry list of OKRs (*https://oreil.ly/UIR2Y*) (objectives and key results) for the coming quarters or a set of external commitments. (No roadmap survives contact with the enemy.) Instead, it signals intention. Roadmaps are invaluable when explaining to stakeholders why urgent but less-important work sometimes has to be deprioritized.

If you're ready to attempt a roadmap, know that every team doing strategic engineering work has one but that it's often in someone's head. Far better to write it down. The act of writing and agreeing on the roadmap document creates better alignment. A lead can draft the document, but the whole team should have an opportunity to give input before adoption.

Roadmaps are living documents and need an update every year or so. Less often than that, you may not be making progress on your strategic goals. Significantly more often than annually, your roadmap may be too focused on the short term.

As Eisenhower said, "What is important is seldom urgent and what is urgent is seldom important." Don't get so bogged down in the day-to-day distractions all SREs face that you neglect planning and executing the long-term projects that will have the greatest impact on your organization.

PART V

The Future of SRE

That 50% Thing

Tanya Reilly

Squarespace

The traditional model for operations was that software engineers would "throw services over the wall" to a dedicated team that would make them work in production. Systems administrators used heroics to keep their sites up while they automated away the jagged edges. Firefighting was just part of the job.

Site reliability brought us a new model. With reliability as a first-class feature, the teams running production expected the same status—and the same salary—as the teams creating the features that ran there. One manifestation of that was the rule that SREs spend no more than 50% of their time on ops work. When I began my first SRE role in 2006, that meant every SRE should spend 50% of their time coding.

However, when you're running services in production, there's always ops work to be done. Something is close to its scaling limits. Something is having mysterious, ephemeral outages. Something is a monster to deploy. SREs who weren't drawn to coding, or who were motivated by solving problems (a common ops personality type) struggled to ignore the interrupts for long enough to ship meaningful coding projects.

Over time, "at least 50% code" became "at most, 50% ops." And, honestly, that's fine. As an industry, we've often over-emphasized (and over-interviewed for) code. It's mature to evolve "50% code" into "50% deliberate project work to make your services better." That still might mean coding, of course, but it also might mean wiring together an off-the-shelf solution, increasing redundancy, or writing documentation.

Thinking beyond code is healthy, but what about the other 50%? Over time, the rule has shifted from "no more than 50% *ops work*" to "no more than 50% *toil*." That feels less healthy to me.

Google's SRE book defines toil as "the kind of work tied to running a production service that tends to be manual, repetitive, automatable, tactical, devoid of enduring value, and that scales linearly as a service grows." Engineers working on operations problems such as performance tuning, monitoring, or scaling will boost their skills as they improve their service. Toil's different. It doesn't change much from week to week, and you rarely learn anything from it. But if you stop doing it, the service will stop working.

Fifty percent ops work sounds like a fine life choice to me. Fifty percent toil doesn't. We're undervaluing SRE skills when we tell other teams that SREs can spend half their time doing work that's repetitive, automatable, tactical, and so on.

Here's a maybe controversial opinion: I don't think SREs should do any more toil than any other engineering discipline. It's fine to fight fires for a little while fixing a crisis, just like we might ask any software engineering team to sprint to get us through a rough time. But that shouldn't be typical. The team of reliability experts should never be a Band-Aid* over systems that can't stay up without repetitive human action. Reduction of toil needs to be an engineering-wide goal, not an SRE hot topic. Reliability and operability can't be an afterthought.

SRE has thrown out a lot of the systems administration hero culture. We're careful to avoid alert fatigue. We're wary of burnout, but we're still far too tolerant of keeping services alive by using toil.

That 50% cap was the right call at the time to distinguish SRE from the operations roles that came before. Now it's time to go further. If SRE wants to take itself seriously as an engineering discipline—and I think it should!—I hope we set more aggressive limits on toil.

Following the Path of Safety-Critical Systems

Heidy Khlaaf

Adelard

SCSs (safety-critical systems) are systems whose failure or malfunction may result in death or serious injury to people, loss or severe damage to equipment or property, and environmental harm. Despite such high risks, SCSs are often riddled with complex software, raising the potential for detrimental behavior. As a result, these systems are subject to stringent regulatory frameworks that require the use of rigorous development techniques that may mitigate adverse behavior.

A prevalent myth within the tech community is that these techniques are unnecessarily rigorous and complex and reserved for only the most critical safety systems. Unfortunately, this means a considerable and rich set of guidance and methodologies developed by the SCS community is seldom used or even considered within the tech industry.

SCSs vary greatly in their requirements regarding the rigor and applicability of development techniques, often overlapping with systems that parallel those within the scope of SRE. For example, IEC 61508, the most prevalent safety standard, consists of methods on how to apply, design, deploy, and maintain safety-related systems. Although this standard may appear specific to only SCSs, a closer examination reveals that the principles mirror those of system dependability used in systems engineering, such as availability, reliability, safety, integrity, and maintainability.

The application of each development approach in IEC 61508 largely depends on the required rigor of the system as defined by an SIL (Safety Integrity Level). An SIL is a measure of an allowable probability that a safety function will fail to respond on demand. SREs may find safety availability—the availability of a safety integrity system to perform a task—looks familiar, described in percentage (%), synonymous to the five-nines high availability requirement, as you can see below.

Safety Integrity Level	Average probability of a dangerous failure on demand of the safety function (PFD)	Safety Availability
SIL 4	$\geq 10^{-5}$ to $< 10^{-4}$ (≥ 1 in 100,000 to < 1 in 10,000)	> 99.99%
SIL 3	$\geq 10^{-4}$ to $< 10^{-3}$ (≥ 1 in 10,000 to < 1 in 1,000)	99.90% to 99.99%
SIL 2	$\geq 10^{-3}$ to $< 10^{-2}$ (≥ 1 in 1,000 to < 1 in 100)	99.00% to 99.90%
SIL 1	$\geq 10^{-2}$ to $< 10^{-1}$ (≥ 1 in 100 to < 1 in 10)	90.00% to 99.00%

Standards such as IEC 61508 thus offer a rich repository of techniques that users can employ to achieve a target SIL, or availability, including requirements traceability, formal methods, static analysis, fault detection, complexity metrics, modular design, defensive programming, MC/DC (modified condition/decision coverage), process simulation, avalanche/stress testing, and many others.

Not all techniques can be applied to or required for all systems, and no distinction between techniques is made across differing requirements. A crucial element of adapting such techniques to SRE is the ability to interpret a standard's requirements against each unique software system. However, such guidance is rarely provided by safety standards, and may require expertise to determine sufficiently when and how to deploy specific development methodologies. As a result, techniques proposed in "The Future of Goal-Based Assurance Cases,"[1] now adopted by the IAEA (International Agency of Atomic Energy),[2] aim to classify the role of how different development methodologies can justify critical system claims such as safety and dependability.

As SRE's relevance continually expands to systems we rely upon daily, the requirements of SREs increasingly align with that of SCSs. Consider safety-critical IoT, where smart medical devices rely on the availability of cloud services to operate at SIL 3. As more software systems intersect with SCS, SREs should look toward SCS disciplines to carve a way forward for the deployment of safe, dependable, and available systems.

---

1 P Bishop, R Bloomfield, and S Guerra, "The future of goal-based assurance cases," in *Proceedings of Workshop on Assurance Cases*, Supplemental Volume of the 2004 International Conference on Dependable Systems and Networks, pp. 390–395 (2004).

2 IAEA Nuclear Energy Series, *Challenges and Approaches for Selecting, Assessing and Qualifying Commercial Industrial Digital Instrumentation and Control Equipment for Use in Nuclear Power Plant Applications* (2020).

Applicable and Achievable Static Analysis

Heidy Khlaaf

Adelard

SA (*static analysis*) is a method of analyzing software properties without executing code and varies in its rigor, encompassing analyses from syntactic checks (e.g., linters) to formal verification techniques. SA can either be manual or automatic, requiring mathematical proofs for the former or automated inspection by static analyzers for the latter.

Generally, static analysis can be categorized by three broad categories, ranked in increasing order of rigor, as follows:

1. Code compliance and metrics analysis

2. Integrity analysis

3. FV (formal verification)

Code compliance checks source code against some set of defined syntactic rules that are deemed to be good practice (*https://www.misra.org.uk*). Tools that support code compliance often include *metric analysis* aimed at assessing code complexity, which includes measures such as:

- Cyclomatic complexity (the number of decision points in a module)
- Path complexity (the number of possible paths through a code module)

Code compliance checkers can build confidence in the quality of the code through identifying poorly constructed code, syntactic nonconformance, or complex control flow that may lead to defects. This can reduce, rather than eliminate, the probability that the code at hand exhibits unexpected behavior.

Generally, static analysis techniques best suited for verifying and validating a software system will depend on factors such as the defined service availability within a SLO/SLA (service level objective or agreement). In this case, code compliance is applicable to all levels of SLO and SLA.

Integrity analysis seeks to ensure that a program never enters a state that is undefined by a programming language. This usually equates to runtime errors, including reading past the end of an array, reading an uninitialized memory location, or dividing by zero. It also considers language-independent defects such as buffer overflows or any concurrency issues that may undermine the correct execution of code (e.g., data race, race conditions, etc.) or that concern interactions between concurrent modules that are unintentional, such as deadlocks.

Integrity analysis is thus the most applicable analysis that can benefit the performance and availability of a system. That is, the removal of common vulnerabilities ensures that a system will perform without unexpected anomalies, especially for systems requiring higher availability (from 99.9% and upward). A system is not functionally correct if there are integrity errors, and integrity analysis can be perceived as a subset of formal verification.

Fortunately, most integrity analysis tools do not require in-depth expertise in either SA or FV, because a plethora of tools can be applied off-the-shelf, automatically and at scale, including Polyspace, CodeSonar, Frama-C, and Facebook Infer.

Formal verification aims to prove functional properties mathematically about a given program against a set of requirements or specifications. It can provide guarantees regarding the behaviors of a system that testing cannot. To do so, a program must first be formalized into a model or abstraction, and a program's functional requirements are then defined in a formal specification language. FV tools thus are typically semi-automated and require expertise in formal methods to form models and specifications.

FV is often only necessary for systems requiring a service availability of 99.99% and upward, because the rigor and manual effort are costly relative to risks averted (see ALARP (*https://oreil.ly/7qbZd*)).

Static analysis and formal verification techniques are underused, given the misconception that they are unnecessarily rigorous and complex. This unfortunately hinders SREs from considering tools that may guide the elimination of burdensome and expensive defects arising in production systems. SREs can likely deploy SA tools with ease and without an overhaul of infrastructure while gaining the system-assurance benefits SA and FV techniques provide.

The Importance of Formal Specification

Hillel Wayne

When dealing with very complex systems, finding bugs becomes much more difficult. Although a wide variety of tools can help you, these tools primarily help identify why a bug has happened. We've done very little as an industry to help you avoid having the bug in the first place.

Why is that? In part, we are still used to thinking of bugs as faults in the code —uncaught nulls, off-by-one, and so on, but the subtlest and most dangerous bugs are problems with the design. They are cases when everything is locally correct but interact in a way that's globally incorrect.

Consider mixing error retries and rolling deployment. The client's initial request and first retry could be handled by different servers running different versions of the code. Any unexpected behavior wouldn't be the fault of the client, server, or load balancer, but arise from the interplay among them.

Nobody has made a mistake. Every local component is doing exactly what we told it to do. Given the complexity of the system, it becomes difficult to understand the consequences of those actions at a global level.

The only way to deal with these is by the hard work of intelligent experts. Us. But just as we have tools to help us write code, we also have tools that help us write designs. One powerful technique is to write a software model of the system and then simulate that model for bugs.

Because we only model the system, not implement it, we can write out a high-level overview in a fraction of the time that it would take to code it all up. Then we can use tools to see whether it satisfies our system requirements. This is called *formal specification*, also known as debuggable designs. Formal specs help you successfully design up front, saving time, money, and sanity.

This could be seen through two examples. By using formal specifications, Amazon was able to find a 35 step bug in DynamoDB (*https://oreil.ly/ XyNUA*) that slipped through extensive design review, code review, and testing. Rackspace applied formal specification late in a project and found a requirements mismatch (*https://oreil.ly/G6y0h*) that required them to redo a year of work. One team writing an embedded operating system found that writing formal specs reduced their overall code size by a factor of ten (*https://oreil.ly/0rToL*).

If formal specification is so powerful, why don't people use it? Mostly for social reasons. Most of the work in formal specification has focused on a few high-priority technologies such as telecommunications and chipsets. As software becomes more critical and increasingly complex over the past half-decade, we've realized its broader potential to benefit software engineers outside of critical systems.

Formal specification does not work miracles. It doesn't write the code for you. It doesn't replace our skills as engineers, but it's a powerful means of finding bugs in our systems before we spend months building them, before we're awoken at 3 a.m. to deal with an outage. You wouldn't build a house without a blueprint. Why would you build a million-dollar system without one?

Risk and Rot in Sociotechnical Systems

Laura Nolan

We work in organizations made up of people, all subject to outcome bias and prone to underestimate or overestimate risks, depending on to what extent normalization of deviance has set in on our team. Executives can become far removed from the reality of life at the front line, and their appreciation of probabilities of adverse events can be strongly affected by recent outcomes.

There is a phenomenon in operations that I've heard called the paradox of preparation—an organization that is effectively managing risks and preventing problems can fail to be recognized as such. Bad outcomes aren't actually occurring because of this preventive work, so decision makers may come to believe that the risks are significantly lower than they actually are. Therefore, leaders may conclude that the organization that is preventing the negative events from occurring isn't an efficient use of resources anymore.

One of the major functions of an SRE or operations team is to manage risks proactively. This kind of work covers a broad spectrum, from keeping systems patched, rotating certs and tokens, and validating backups, to less-routine things like writing runbooks and recovery tools, running disaster tests, performing production readiness reviews for new systems, and doing thorough reviews of near-miss production incidents. These are also the kinds of work that can fall by the wayside all too easily when a team is overloaded or understaffed. The eventual outcome is likely to be a crisis and the start of a new cycle of investment.

An important part of our job, therefore, is to make the value of our work visible to avoid the organizational rot that makes us underestimate risk and underinvest in reliability. We live in a data-driven world, but, of course, we can't track the incidents that don't happen because of good preventive work. However, at times when we aren't in crisis mode, we can do many other things to show how our work contributes to increasing reliability.

We can create internal SLOs for the routine jobs we do to manage risks and set up dashboards to show whether we're meeting those SLOs. Write production-readiness standards that you'd like your services to meet, covering areas such as change management, monitoring and alerting, load balancing and request management, failover, and capacity planning. Track how your services meet those standards (or don't). Set up chaos engineering and game days to test how your services deal with failure and track those results as you would postmortem action items. Load test your systems to understand how they scale and address bottlenecks you will encounter in the next year or two. Take near misses and surprises seriously and track them along with action items. All these things help prevent a slide into normalization of deviance as well as giving visibility into our work.

As engineers, we have a responsibility to communicate clearly about risks in our systems and the proactive work we do to reduce them. However, the fish rots from the head down; engineering leaders ultimately make critical decisions. Therefore, they must be acutely aware of outcome bias and the risk of disconnects in understanding of risk between front-line engineers and themselves. Most important, they must be mindful of the crisis–complacency cycle and maintain an appropriate continuous investment in resilience and reliability to avoid crisis.

SRE in Crisis

Niall Murphy

Microsoft

Inflamed race relations (*https://oreil.ly/OFuCX*) leading to widespread riots. New startups (*https://oreil.ly/jhtgm*) in Silicon Valley. Virulent anti-immigration feeling (*https://oreil.ly/HT2Ow*) stoked in the UK. A lethal pandemic, coming from Asia (*https://oreil.ly/GLOPz*). It sounds like today, but it was 1968.

In Germany, a younger, smaller NATO, then on the cutting edge of computing, held what has a good claim to be the first software engineering conference in history. (*https://oreil.ly/eEjZg*) In keeping with the state of the world at the time, the conference declared a crisis (*https://oreil.ly/rHoso*): our ability to write high-quality software, functioning reliably, was under strain as machines became more powerful and complexity grew.

One of those recognizing the crisis was the young computer scientist Edsger Dijkstra, who wrote (*https://oreil.ly/idraB*), "The design of any large sophisticated system is going to be a very difficult job, and whenever one meets people responsible for such undertakings, one finds them very much concerned about the reliability issue, and rightly so."

His solution was to push for consistency, discipline, and rigor in programming. This led to approaches now considered foundational—structured programming, for example—although, as with all novelty, initially treated with suspicion. In honor of Dijkstra, then, I declare the same: SRE is in crisis. Our old approaches will not solve it.

Let's face it, most of what we have in the profession as templates for behavior or reasoning about systems relies on a body of knowledge with little evidence to back it up. Four years after publication of the SRE book (*https://oreil.ly/_omO2*), many in the profession are still effectively copying and pasting their standard operating procedures from the pages of that book, understandably but wrongly.

I look around and I see not much that would pass for rigor in our profession. Dijkstra's own pioneering work on the foundations of distributed systems—

semaphores, mutexes, self-stabilization, and many others—is perhaps the closest we have, but it is only for the computer science side of what we do. Much that we do in SRE is outside of that context—perhaps even most of it—yet we generally have unquestioned lore and (at best) rules of thumb as a basis for that work.

A few examples:

- Why is the toil-to-project work ratio 50:50? Is that the right number, rather than 20:80, or indeed having no fixed ratio but a flexible approach?

- Do we have any way to understand why system-level changes (e.g., to microservice meshes) should be successful, other than trying them and seeing?

- If SLOs are such a good model, what do we do (*https://oreil.ly/xqVIM*) when one sufficiently bad incident destroys an error budget for an entire year?

In many ways, the problems of 1968 are the problems of today—foremost of which is complexity. Complexity will kill us. Indeed, it is killing us today (*https://oreil.ly/Iui76*), and we seem to have no defense that works—other than a holistic practice that SRE aspires to but very often falls short of.

In 1968, A. G. Fraser of the Cambridge Mathematical Laboratory said: "I just want to make the point that reliability really is a design issue, in the sense that unless you are conscious of the need for reliability throughout the design, you might as well give up." The promise of SRE is precisely that; I do not see it fulfilled.

Treat it with suspicion if you must, but perhaps this, too, will come to be seen as the beginning of an inevitable realization: we don't know what we're doing, or why it works, or even whether it works—and yet it is more important than ever to get it right. Otherwise, our 1968 will end up looking like 1986 (*https://oreil.ly/QZgcQ*).

Expected Risk Limitations

Blake Bisset

Microsoft Azure

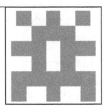

I've generally employed two major risk analysis methodologies.

The first is architectural analysis. This is typically looking at perceived or unrealized risk through some flavor of FMA (failure mode analysis): FMEA (failure mode and effects analysis), FMECA (failure mode, effects, and criticality analysis), or even just a basic folks-sitting-at-a-whiteboard session looking for common anti-patterns in the design of the system and jotting them down, like lack of circuit breaking, throttling, exponential backoff and retry, jitter—that kind of stuff. These can be purely qualitative and subjective and still have value, but they also rely heavily on what you already know about your system. Or, rather, on the mental map of your system and what you *think* you know about it.

The second is data-driven analysis, when we add historical reliability data from realized risk to the FMA process (failure modes, effects, and diagnostic analysis [FMEDA]) or build heat maps of contributing factors for outages across a number of dimensions—such as type of failure, services involved, and geography—and associate them with user impact based on degradation, number of affected users, and duration.

The goal here is to arrive at an annualized (or other periodic) expectation of the realized impact of a particular risk. These are short essays, so I won't go into the details of any of these methodologies, since an internet search should put you on the right path quickly. You can pick as simple or complex a risk-modeling structure as you need, based on how much complexity you're dealing with and how much of the low-hanging fruit you've already knocked off the branches of your system. The internet will provide. Probably. After all, it's a complex system, too, and prone to its own emergent failure conditions.

Building these kinds of data maps can help us find what our best areas for investment are, not only for the things that are our top "root causes," but also for the kinds of problems that aren't the leading contributor to most or even many outages but have a contributing role in many of them. In the past, I've been able to tease out things like how a frustrating throttling system that everyone thought was good enough not to invest in replacing was actually the seventh most common contributing factor to downtime at our company, even though it was only identified as the "root cause" in less than 2% of incidents.

This approach is powerful as well, but like the architectural one, it, too, is limited. Data-driven analysis can only give us this kind of investment guidance about the problems that we already in some degree know we have. Or should know anyway. They're already in our risk registry—things we've seen before and likely have seen relatively frequently if a solid, quantifiable history of realized risk is associated with them.

Where the approach struggles to deliver an annualized expected risk is in dealing with known but unquantifiable risks: the things we enter in the risk registry because we think they're probably not good or will be a problem someday but which we can't actually characterize with any data.

As a result, we can have trouble deciding how to balance the work required to fix them against features and other more measurable tech debt, or funding the project and defending the work against such competing priorities even if we ourselves believe it to be critical. The approach breaks down entirely on the actual black swans (or electrified pelicans) and unknown unknowns.

Much like our esteemed editors' content length rules, however, I think there is a way to get past this limitation. So I'll tell you about it in the next installment!

Beyond Local Risk: Accounting for Angry Birds

Blake Bisset

Microsoft Azure

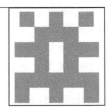

Data-driven analysis can only provide the kind of engineering investment guidance we want when applied to problems we already know we have—or should know, anyway. They're already in our risk registry: things we've seen before and likely have seen relatively frequently if we actually associate a solid, quantifiable history of realized risk with them.

In dealing with known but unquantifiable risks, or the actual black swans and unknown unknowns, our best efforts often fail us, and we quickly reach a place where we need help in the divine or psychotherapeutic sense. Or possibly both.

These things will almost never turn up in our data until it's too late, or if they do, they will still not be amenable to actual calculations of risk and predicted impact and cost over time. Although all these things are critical tools in the life of an engineer, they're not inherently reliable, or at least not very likely to produce the kind of evidence that will convince a plurality of VPs to impose a Code Yellow.

This is where things get interesting, however. Over the course of building taxonomies of failure at a few companies, I've become very interested in the idea of expanding this mechanism beyond a single division or organization. What might we be able to achieve with a broader shared taxonomy and data pool? What if we started to treat system failure like an underwriting project? Actually to build an industry-standard database of failure types and frequency in different kinds of systems?

What might be achieved from a data-sharing standpoint if the taxonomy of contributing factors and failure patterns that we'd developed to apply to our own incident reports, and used to good effect internally, were instead replaced by an open-standard taxonomy and measurement system that could be used to generate and gather data across many organizations?

If we apply a common taxonomy to these events across the industry and develop shared incident reporting, combined with that taxonomy of contributing factors and quantified impact, the quality of the data set we have to use for pattern generation and frequency–risk projection changes considerably. What is infrequent for a single provider, even at massive scale, might become discernible across a number of them. We might begin to shift some of those known unquantifiable risks to predictable ones or even transform some of the locally unknown unknowns into known patterns of failure, against which we can take reasonable precautions in proportion to their annualized expected impact.

The answer to our unmeasurable or unknown unknowns is the same one that faced the electrical industry and consumer electronics back when they were at their early stages, as the computing sector is today. As an industry, we can aim to build for our information systems what is essentially the same kind of actuarial tables used for our physical systems.

We're already predicting the likelihood that an insurer will have to pay out on a policy due to electrical fires if there is a certain mix of components and wiring code implementations in our offices. We may be able to do the same for determining how important it is to implement production canary testing on a pipeline compared to a relational database, or the average annual expectation of power outage minutes due to a transformer at our data center vaporizing a large bird, or even the reliability impact of the relative proportion of your infrastructure engineers who use Vim versus Emacs. Now that would be interesting.

Then again, some questions are likely dangerous to try to answer.

A Word from Software Safety Nerds

J. Paul Reed

Netflix

Any SRE tasked with the care and feeding of even the most modest of services will, inevitably, have a Bad Day™. After the incident plays out, we find ourselves party to a postmortem. Operational retrospectives—a more accurate name for what we software developers and operations engineers practice, unless your outage resulted in *actual death*—are likely not new to you. What may be news is the interest in the concept of safety and the mechanics of how we learn from incidents in software as individuals, teams, and whole organizations.

Following are a few insights we software safety nerds have uncovered and are actively studying, attempting to help us all learn more from these impactful events:

Leaning into complexity
> The rise of web-scale distributed systems over the past 15 years has renewed interest in understanding the true impact of complexity science on our field. Many SREs throw the word around colloquially, but it was Mark Burgess's configuration management work, described in *In Search of Certainty*, that laid the groundwork for us to consider that our systems, especially in the cloud, have more in common with quantum physics than with physics grounded in equal-and-opposite, cause-and-effect reactions.

The implications of quantum
> Once we accept the true nature of the complexity of our systems, this calls into question a host of models and methods we've traditionally relied on in incident analysis; suddenly, linear models are woefully ill-suited to describe incidents. Once linearity falls, so too do "root cause," "Five Whys," and best practices. This can be jarring, but the complex world we operate in has no use for such concepts.

Reimagining of blame

How many incidents has your team attributed to "human error?" A complex world without linearity also requires us to eschew the concept of human error as an explanation for incidents. Fundamentally, it serves as a proxy for "the point at which we decided to stop asking questions." A rise in blameless retrospectives is one implementation, but because blame is an ingrained human reaction to stress, the focus is moving from lack of blame, an impossible order, toward blame-aware, when we acknowledge blame's presence (often by engineers *blaming themselves!*) and seek to move past it in a productive way during our incident analyses.

The people of our systems

The addition of the modifier "sociotechnical" to the description of our complex systems has increased, too. It acknowledges that SRE work is not solely pushing code, shepherding data, and keeping bits happy and machines fed. This work is done by people, and it's people who directly contribute to the successes and failures of that system in ways we have discounted for far too long. We need to change that if we truly want to improve those systems.

The cultivation of expertise

Finally, this movement is challenging the notion that the sole purpose of incident analysis is to brainstorm, document, and enact remediation items. These are important, but the real value for improvement is *the cultivation of expertise in ourselves and each other*, not a tuned alert or additional unit test. The latter solves the incident we had; the former will solve the next incident we'll have.

Safety science has a lot to teach SREs about how to improve our work and the reliability of the systems we care for, but it is a new framing of the problem, and that can be understandably uncomfortable. Reach out to the growing crew of safety and reliability nerds in the SRE space; the only thing you have to lose are those late-night pages that make us *all* miserable.

Incidents: A Window into Gaps

Lorin Hochstein

Netflix

Incidents force us to confront the reality that our systems don't always behave as we expect. It's an uncomfortable feeling, and we want to have faith that this won't happen again. To renew that faith after an incident, we work to determine why the system broke, but we can learn more from incidents than just how to prevent a repeat. We can identify a range of *gaps*—deficiencies that we can potentially address—that exist inside our organizations.

One kind of gap we can recognize is a *tooling* gap, when we see engineers having trouble using operational tools. For example, we can identify when engineers struggle to make sense of feedback from a tool during an incident, or when they make an error using a tool to make a production change. In particular, whenever we notice a *workaround*, someone performing a task the wrong way, that's a clue there's a tooling gap. Information about tooling gaps should be fed back to the owners of these operational tools.

Another kind of gap is an *operational expertise* gap. This is when engineers are missing important operational skills they need to do their jobs effectively. Perhaps a certain graph on a dashboard was always wrong, because the engineer who created it didn't fully understand the metrics query language. It was only after the incident that somebody noticed. An operational expertise gap can develop over time, since our systems are constantly undergoing change. The policy you used when configuring autoscaling may have been the recommended approach last year, but it's now deprecated.

Last, there are *resource* gaps, when a team doesn't have enough resources to handle their workload. There are two reasons to worry about resource gaps. One is the law of stretched systems: every system will eventually be pushed to its capacity. Imagine an individual team that's running at capacity and receives additional headcount. When they hire someone new, they'll have some slack. Inevitably, though, the team will keep taking on more work until they're running at capacity again.

The other challenge with resource gaps is the law of fluency. This is the phenomenon when a skilled engineer can gracefully handle some amount of work overload, and they give no indication that they are working beyond capacity ("I'm doing fine!") until they become completely overwhelmed. You can see the law of fluency in action when engineers feel the need to switch between different tasks to get all of their work done, such as monitoring a complex deployment, responding to internal support requests, and doing development work. This overload increases both the risk of errors and the risk of burnout on the team. Burnout can lead to team members leaving, increasing the load on the team even further. The earlier we identify a team at risk of overload, the less costly it is for the organization to address the problem.

Each person inside an organization has only a partial understanding of how the overall system works. Every time an incident happens, we have the opportunity to learn about the gaps that the incident exposes. By highlighting these gaps, we can begin to prepare for the future.

The Third Age of SRE

Björn "Beorn" Rabenstein

Grafana Labs

In the first age, SRE was proprietary to Google, and knowledge about it left the company only by diffusion.

In the second age, SRE was set free. *Site Reliability Engineering* (*https://oreil.ly/n0pxP*) (O'Reilly) in 2016 made blatantly obvious that a fundamental change was happening from a weirdly named department within Google to a generally known profession. The fittingly named SREcon has happened regularly and increasingly successfully since 2014. In the job market, SRE is a downright buzzword, appearing in résumés and job descriptions everywhere.

The incredible popularity of SRE makes me believe we have reached the late stage of the second age, and its conclusion will be marked by an interesting inversion of the current hiring hype: the end of the dedicated SRE role as we know it.

How? During the second age, many organizations quickly realized that their much smaller size prevented them from performing SRE exactly like Google. Even an organization large enough to maintain a dedicated SRE team—most couldn't—usually came to the conclusion that they couldn't just hire a certain number of SREs to do "that SRE thing." Instead, every engineer had to become a part-time SRE. David N. Blank-Edelman's *Seeking SRE* (*https://oreil.ly/EgtxD*) (O'Reilly, 2018) documents a number of those stories, including (shameless plug) my own witness account as a production engineer at SoundCloud.

From that perspective, the high demand for SREs in the work market is mostly driven by the desire to find someone to spread SRE knowledge among the other engineers. An organization that has truly arrived in the third age is one where that has already happened. All engineers can wear an SRE hat as part of their job, and at least smaller organizations will then stop hiring dedicated SREs. Instead, an SRE mindset will be an important hiring requirement for every engineering role.

What *necessitates* those transitions between ages, you may ask? For the second age, it was the democratization and proliferation of cloud-native technologies. The very insightful definition published by the CNCF (*https:// oreil.ly/HIOp3*) showed that cloud-native technologies allowed even small organizations quickly to reach a level of complexity and scale at which SRE becomes a necessity.

For the third age, it will be the optimization of the portion of engineers who work in a dedicated SRE role rather than directly on the actual product. An organization at second-age maturity, where most engineers act as part-time SREs, will realize that most of the tasks of the remaining dedicated SREs could be handed over to service providers, including but not limited to traditional infrastructure-focused cloud providers. In fact, the increasing selection of higher-order services, which run on top of other cloud services, will drive most of the opportunity growth.

There is a trade-off, of course. The larger an organization, the more efficient it is to run a larger part of its stack on its own, but with the steady innovation of the service providers, the bar is moving up here.

Will we soon enjoy "SRE as a service" so we can completely forget about operational concerns? On the contrary. In a second-age scenario, it is actually easier for engineers to get away with a certain amount of operational ignorance by relying on SREs within the organization. In the third age, most engineers will be very close to production, enabled by the SRE-inspired tools and services at their fingertips. To use those effectively, they will require an SRE mindset.

The unimaginable power of SRE in the third age is that it will (and has to) be in everyone's head. The moment universities include SRE classes in their computer science programs will be a sure sign that the third age has begun.

Contributors

Kurt Andersen

Kurt Andersen is part of the Product-SRE team at LinkedIn. He has been one of the co-chairs for SREcon Americas and active in the anti-abuse community for over 20 years. Kurt has spoken around the world on various aspects of reliability, authentication, anti-abuse, and security and co-authored *What Is SRE?* (*https://oreil.ly/d_HOC*) (O'Reilly). He also works on internet standards through the IETF and serves on the USENIX Board of Directors and as liaison to the SREcon conferences worldwide.

Daria Barteneva

Daria Barteneva is currently Senior Software Engineer in Observability Platform in Azure. With a background in applied mathematics, artificial intelligence, and music, Daria is passionate about data mining, diversity in tech, and opera. In her current role, Daria is focused on changing organizational culture, processes, and platform to improve service reliability and on-call experience. Daria is originally from Moscow, Russia, spent 20 years in Portugal, and now lives in Dublin, Ireland.

Jacob Bednarz

Jacob Bednarz is a snowboarding woodworker who during the day attempts to build reliable systems out of unreliable components. He is currently at Envato, spending his days on open source, performance, security, and reliability issues as a site reliability engineer. He irregularly rants at *https://jacobbednarz.com*.

Fewer Spreadsheets, More Napkins, page 125

Bouke van der Bijl

Bouke van der Bijl is a software engineer who is always thinking about the bigger picture. He has experience creating and scaling new products at Shopify and DigitalOcean. In his free time, he reads a lot of books and does training and coaching for the Dutch Informatics Olympiad, helping high school kids excel at competitive programming. You can find him online at *https://bou.ke*.

There Is No Magic, page 18

Blake Bisset

Blake Bisset got his first legal tech job at 16. Now he's allowed to make shaky-fists at the cloud. A startup with a bunch of kids wondering why they couldn't watch movies on the internet led him to Google, where he broke enough things eventually to win go/bestpostmortem and leave. Then, as head of Reliability Engineering at Dropbox, he lost a bet with Niall Murphy and now stacks turtles in the reliability mines at Azure.

Expected Risk Limitations, page 193
Beyond Local Risk: Accounting for Angry Birds, page 195

Johnny Boursiquot

Johnny Boursiquot is a multi-disciplined software engineer with over two decades of experience and a love for teaching and community-building. He stays busy as a trainer, speaker, and diversity advocate within the Go programming language community, where he also frequently serves as podcast host, user group organizer, and conference program committee member. He is a site reliability engineer at Salesforce's Heroku while also leading engineering at a burgeoning startup.

Fatema Boxwala

Fatema Boxwala is an engineer who hates code and computers. If she could, she would spend all her time cooking, eating, and making mediocre art. She's given the occasional talk at conferences like LISA and SREcon, but lately she's been more involved in the program committees for these conferences. She lives in Seattle with her personal demons and her roommate, Kelly. Follow her at *https://twitter.com/fatty_box*.

Michelle Brush

Michelle Brush is a math geek turned computer geek with 20 years of software development experience. She has developed algorithms and data structures for pathfinding, search, compression, and data processing in embedded as well as distributed systems. In her current role as an SRE Manager for Google, she leads teams of SREs that ensure GCP's APIs are reliable. Previously, she served as an Engineering Director for Cerner Corporation, responsible for the data processing platform for Cerner's Population Health solutions. Before that role, she was the lead engineer for Garmin's automotive routing algorithm. She is a huge fan of tardigrades.

Miles Bryant

Miles Bryant is a platform engineer at Monzo, a bank changing the way people interact with money. He's been on the first-line on-call rota for 2 years, dealing with many late-night pages, driving forward improvements and in general trying to make on-call great. His interests include distributed systems, sleeping well at night, outdoor sports, and PC strategy games.

Effortless Incident Management, page 82
On-Call Rotations that People Want to Join, page 144
The Power of Uniformity, page 164

Karla Burnett

Karla Burnett spends her days figuring out how to make systems do things they shouldn't and then preventing them from doing just that again. She's currently a staff engineer working on security at Stripe and, away from work, an avid crafter and plane enthusiast.

Get Your Work Recognized: Write a Brag Document, page 71

Kristine Chen

Kristine Chen is a staff software engineer at Google and former SRE. During her time as an SRE, she brought SRE principles and best practices to mobile applications. A graduate of U.C. Berkeley, she is best known for revolutionizing Google's internal monitoring strategy and pioneering methods of supporting mobile device reliability remotely. In her free time, she likes to read, play video games, and hang out with her corgi.

Holistic Approach to Product Reliability, page 107

Anita Clarke

Anita Clarke's 14-year career as an award-winning Software Quality Assurance professional and a 10+ year fashion blogging career converged to her current path as an engineering storyteller. As the Senior Managing Editor of Shopify's Engineering blog and writer, she brings her technical editor expertise to help developers craft and share their stories about their work. She's shared her technology journey with DevTO, ITAC Inspiring Tech Careers Conference, and TD Then and Now. @geekigirl *https://www.engineeringstoryteller.ca*

Storytelling Is a Superpower, page 69
Make Your Engineering Blog a Priority, page 168

Nati Cohen

Nati Cohen is a production engineer at Here Technologies and a teaching assistant at the Interdisciplinary Center Herzliya. Previous experience includes: operations consulting, software development, *nix administration, and security research in the Intelligence Corps as well as in multiple startup companies.

Methodological Debugging, page 61

Narayan Desai

Narayan Desai is an SRE at Google, where he focuses on the reliability of Google Cloud Platform Data Analytics products. He has a checkered past, having worked on scheduling, configuration management, supercomputers, and metagenomics—always in the context of production systems.

When SLOs Attack: Pathological SLOs and How to Fix Them, page 105

Ingrid Epure

Ingrid Epure wants to make the world simpler, one production system at a time. She talks and cares deeply about tech culture and believes it should be more accessible and open. Ingrid is an international speaker and part of the SREcon EMEA program committee. When she is not busy being a senior engineer at Netlify, she reads a lot, learns to draw, builds mechanical keyboards, and nerds out about coffee and music.

You Don't Know for Sure Until It Runs in Production, page 97
In Search of the Lost Time, page 109

Chris Evans

Chris Evans is the Platform Team lead at Monzo, a bank changing the way people interact with their money. His team is responsible for building and operating the Monzo platform, covering everything from its physical data centers and networking through to the container scheduling platform and microservice deployment tooling. Since he joined in March 2018, Monzo has grown by more than four million customers and added over 1,000 new microservices to production.

Effortless Incident Management, page 82
On-Call Rotations that People Want to Join, page 144
The Power of Uniformity, page 164

Julia Evans

Julia Evans is a software engineer and writer who loves weird bugs and helping people learn how computers work. She was a staff engineer at Stripe, where she worked on networking infrastructure and machine learning. She now runs Wizard Zines, where she writes and publishes tiny books that teach computing fundamentals. You can find her at *https://jvns.ca*.

Why You Should Understand (a Little) About TCP, page 22
Get Your Work Recognized: Write a Brag Document, page 71

Liz Fong-Jones

Liz Fong-Jones is a developer advocate, labor and ethics organizer, and Site Reliability Engineer (SRE) with 16+ years of experience. She is an advocate at Honeycomb for the SRE and Observability communities, and previously was an SRE working on products ranging from the Google Cloud Load Balancer to Google Flights.

Observability in the Development Cycle, page 16
The Role of Cardinality, page 28

Lucas Fontes

A black hat in another life, Lucas Fontes helped shape the internet in Brazil in the late '90s by building ISPs in remote areas and helping scale the biggest dial-up provider in the country with over 20 million accounts. In 2018, he bootstrapped the DigitalOcean Kubernetes team and is now focused on improving Auth0's Platform offering. Always Rushing B, Lucas is also an avid FPS player.

Security Is like an Onion, page 30

Dr. Nicole Forsgren

Dr. Nicole Forsgren is the VP of Research and Strategy at GitHub. She is author of the Shingo Publication Award–winning book, *Accelerate: The Science of Lean Software and DevOps* (IT Revolution Press), and is best known as lead investigator on the largest DevOps studies to date. She has been a successful entrepreneur (with an exit to Google), professor, performance engineer, and sysadmin. Her work has been published in several peer-reviewed journals.

The Best Advice I Can Give to Teams, page 136

Elise Gale

Elise Gale is a Senior Software Engineer on the Azure Observability Platform team at Microsoft. She has spent the last five years working on metrics and telemetry. Past projects include the alerting engine and query service used internally for Microsoft Azure critical metrics. Her current focus is infrastructure and on-call health. Outside of work, she enjoys hiking, biking, and reading a good book. She holds a B.S. in Computer Science from the University of Wisconsin–Madison.

Legendary, page 101

Felix Glaser

Felix Glaser is a Berlin transplant to Canada. He deeply cares about securing computer systems of any kind. If he's not coding, you can find Felix mountain biking and climbing in the Canadian Rockies.

To All the SREs I've Loved, page 131

Jason Hand

Jason Hand works as a senior cloud advocate at Microsoft, enabling others to build systems safely and sustainably in the cloud. Co-host of "All Around Azure" and "The Community Pulse," Jason educates others on current principles and practices of building highly available systems and performs the role of developer relations in those efforts. Author of numerous books and articles on modern web operations, Jason enjoys sharing his expertise and guidance to learn and improve continuously.

Unpacking the On-Call Divide, page 78

Alex Hidalgo

Alex Hidalgo is the principal site reliability engineer at Nobl9 and author of *Implementing Service Level Objectives* (*https://oreil.ly/C3tL8*) (O'Reilly, September 2020). During his career, he has developed a deep love for sustainable operations, proper observability, and using SLO data to drive discussions and make decisions. Alex's previous jobs have included IT support, network security, restaurant work, t-shirt design, and hosting game shows at bars. When not sharing his passion for technology with others, you can find him scuba diving or watching college basketball. He lives in Brooklyn with his partner Jen and a rescue dog named Taco. Alex has a BA in philosophy from Virginia Commonwealth University.

Site Reliability Engineering in Six Words, page 2
The Reliability Stack, page 10
I Have an Error Budget—Now What?, page 57

Lorin Hochstein

Lorin Hochstein is a senior software engineer on the Delivery Orchestration team at Netflix. He was previously senior software engineer at SendGrid Labs, lead architect for Cloud Services at Nimbis Services, computer scientist at the University of Southern California's Information Sciences Institute, and assistant professor in the Department of Computer Science and Engineering at the University of Nebraska–Lincoln. Lorin has a B.Eng. in computer engineering from McGill University, an MS in electrical engineering from Boston University, and a PhD in computer science from the University of Maryland.

Making Work Visible, page 74
Incidents: A Window into Gaps, page 199

Matthew Huxtable

Matthew Huxtable is a practitioner and technical leader with deep experience as a software engineer, systems administrator, and SRE. His interests lie where deep systems understanding meets human factors in the quest for reliable systems that users love to use. He's a lifelong technologist with experience in startups, enterprises, and running his own small businesses. Matthew holds two degrees in computer science from the University of Cambridge and is currently lead SRE at a UK-based neobank.

SRE, at Any Size, Is Cultural, page 45
Everyone Is an SRE in a Small Organization, page 47

Avishai Ish-Shalom

In a world where anything has an API, and everything is a software problem, this insight has guided Avishai Ish-Shalom throughout his diverse career, working on improving the complex sociotechnical systems that create and operate modern software and promoting the use of mathematics in system design and operations. After spending 15 years in various software fields and capacities, Avishai has served as engineer in residence at Aleph VC, engineering manager at *Wix.com*, co-founder of Fewbytes, and consultant to many other companies on software operations, reliability, design, and culture. Currently, Avishai spends his time as an independent researcher exploring the application of complexity science to software engineering.

Methodological Debugging, page 61

Shubheksha Jalan

Shubheksha Jalan is a software engineer keenly interested in complex problems at the intersection of distributed systems, reliability, and infrastructure at scale. She enjoys breaking down hard technical concepts through doodles, illustrations, and easy-to-understand blog posts. When she's not too busy fighting computers, she enjoys being outdoors and doing arts and crafts.

Trading Places: SRE and Product, page 172

Heidy Khlaaf

Heidy Khlaaf is a senior research consultant at Adelard LLP, where she evaluates, specifies, and verifies the implementations of safety-critical systems. She received her PhD from University College London, where she developed novel research methodologies, in part with Microsoft Research, to automate fully the verification of temporal properties over software systems.

Following the Path of Safety-Critical Systems, page 183
Applicable and Achievable Static Analysis, page 185

Justin Li

It was rumored that Justin Li's first words as a baby were "production excellence." The phrase, for Justin, could easily apply both to distributed systems and music; he's just as happy to talk about performance sharding as he is about proto-future-funk. At Shopify, he is a staff production engineer. If you were able to buy a lip kit during a massive flash sale, or to ride a go-kart in headquarters, he helped make that happen.

Thinking About Resilience, page 14

Spike Lindsey

Spike Lindsey is a senior production engineer who has wrangled many large distributed systems at companies, including Shopify and Monzo. He believes that on-call rotations can and should be humane and sustainable. When not holding a pager, he plays in a string of endless failed metal bands and enjoys whisky.

If You're Doing Runbooks, Do Them Well, page 84
Optimize for MTTBTB (Mean Time to Back to Bed), page 148

John Looney

John Looney has been an SRE since 2005, managing most types of large distributed systems for Google and Facebook. He has been teaching people to be an SRE for more than 10 years, and is on the SREcon steering committee. He is now a production engineering manager, supporting the people who deploy firmware and operating systems to Facebook's fleet. He hopes to ensure that open system firmware will be firmware, built for SRE by SRE.

Don't Take Advice from Graybeards, page 40
Don't Let Anyone Run Code in Your Context, page 170

Lei Lopez

Lei Lopez is a site reliability engineer based in Montreal, Canada. She previously worked on building tools for incident response as well as for tracking and improving the quality of production systems at Shopify. Instead of climbing or baking artisanal bread, she likes to do improv comedy, watch pro wrestling, and read through mountains of library books.

Heroes Are Necessary, but Hero Culture Is Not, page 142

Andrew Louis

Andrew Louis is a senior software engineer at DigitalOcean, where he works on building out DigitalOcean's constantly growing stack of networking products. Prior to that, he worked at Shopify as a production engineer, hardening the storefront asset delivery pipeline, and supercharging last-mile content delivery. Andrew is an unapologetic Drake stan and an avid open-source enthusiast.

Rita Lu

Rita Lu is a senior site reliability engineer at Google, where she currently works on large-scale serving infrastructure for YouTube, with a focus on capacity management. She enjoys solving systems problems and finding creative ways to run software in the most efficient way possible while respecting SLOs. Previously, she has worked at Shopify. When she's not developing stuff or looking at graphs, she likes to read, ride her motorcycle, do yoga, and play the piano.

Charity Majors

Charity Majors is the CTO and co-founder of honeycomb.io, previously with Parse, Facebook, and Linden Lab, and an operations engineer by trade. Peat is life. Code is the enemy. Why do I always end up responsible for the databases?

Caitie McCaffrey

Caitie McCaffrey is a Backend Brat and Distributed Systems diva. She currently is the architect and developer manager of the Azure Sphere Security Services, where she's working to secure IoT devices. Caitie has spent her career building large-scale services and systems at Twitter, 343 Industries,

Microsoft Game Studios, and HBO. She has credits on several video games, including *Gears of War 2*, *Gears of War 3*, *Halo 4*, and *Halo 5*.

On-Call Health: The Metric You Could Be Measuring, page 152
Helping Leaders Prioritize On-Call Health, page 154

Tamara Miner

Tamara Miner has worked on infrastructure and developer tools for more than 14 years in the United States and Europe. She is currently the engineering manager of Improbable's Partner Engineering team in London. Previously, Tamara launched multiple SaaS products for London startups, Riot Games, and Microsoft Azure Services. She is a recipient of the Forbes 30 Under 30 and the Microsoft Xbox Women in Gaming Rising Star awards. She loves food and robots and spends her spare time tinkering with both.

How Startups Can Build an SRE Mindset, page 63
Unexpected Lessons from Office Hours, page 111

Effie Mouzeli

Effie Mouzeli studied physics and distributed scientific computing but didn't turn out to be a physicist or a scientific computer scientist. She has worked as a systems engineer/SRE at a number of startups and small organizations (most of which are not with us anymore), where her responsibilities were usually in automation and infrastructure architecture and working closely with developers. Currently, she is on the SRE team that takes care of Wikipedia and its sister projects at the Wikimedia Foundation.

How Wikipedia Is Served to You, page 20
The Human Baseline in SRE, page 117

Arshia Mufti

Arshia Mufti is an infrastructure software engineer from Kashmir, living in Toronto.

Bytes per User Value, page 166

Brian Murphy

Brian Murphy is a Site Reliability Engineering Manager working for G-Research in London, UK. He has spent the last 4 years on his SRE journey, doing every job from solo SRE to building and managing SRE teams. He gave his first public talk at SREcon EMEA 2019, and he focuses his positive attitude and energy into organizational and cultural change.

Metrics Are Not SLIs (The Measure Everything Trap), page 103

Niall Murphy

Niall Murphy is a senior lead in Azure site reliability engineering for Microsoft. He is the instigator, co-author, and co-editor of the best-selling, award-winning *Site Reliability Engineering* (*https://oreil.ly/0nWyn*) (O'Reilly, 2016) and numerous other papers, talks, and books. He is probably one of the few people in the world to hold degrees in computer science, mathematics, and poetry studies. He lives in Dublin with his wife and two special-needs children; for fun, he does landscape photography (*http://www.edgecases.photos*).

Do We Know Why We Really Want Reliability?, page 4
SRE in Crisis, page 191

Daniella Niyonkuru

Daniella Niyonkuru is a production engineer at Shopify, where she builds a better, faster, and more resilient platform. Projects she has worked on include disaster recovery tools, data corruption detection, and incident management tooling. Before entering the SRE world, Daniella was an aircraft system software specialist and researched formal model-driven development for embedded systems.

Integrating Empathy into SRE Tools, page 90
Using ChatOps to Implement Empathy, page 93

Laura Nolan

Laura Nolan is a serial part-time master's degree student and SRE tech lead who enjoys making both distributed systems and teams work better. In her spare (ha!) time, she writes a regular column for ;login: magazine. She is a senior staff engineer at Slack in Dublin, Ireland.

Complex: The Most Overloaded Word in Technology, page 133
Important but Not Urgent: Roadmaps for SREs, page 178
Risk and Rot in Sociotechnical Systems, page 189

Joan O'Callaghan

Joan O'Callaghan is the Site Operations Lead at Udemy. She has worked in SRE and Incident Management (in one form or another) for 14 years. Iterative improvements are her favorite thing. She likes to host and write blameless postmortems and take long walks on the beach where she has imaginary arguments with people that don't like reliability as much as she does.

Auditing Your Environment for Improvements, page 49
How to Change Things, page 59

Todd Palino

Todd Palino is a senior staff engineer in site reliability at LinkedIn on the Capacity Engineering team, where his team is creating a framework for application capacity measurement, analysis, and change intelligence. Prior to that, he was responsible for architecture, day-to-day operations, and tools development for one of the largest Apache Kafka deployments. He is also the co-author of *Kafka: The Definitive Guide* (*https://oreil.ly/XWPmr*) (O'Reilly). Out of the office, you can find him at conferences like SREcon and LISA, sharing his experience from years in SRE technical leadership. Or maybe out on the trails, training for the next marathon.

It's Okay Not to Know, and It's Okay to Be Wrong, page 67

Eva Parish

Eva Parish has worked as a technical writer for the past eight years, creating documentation for a variety of audiences, including developers, system administrators, and nontechnical end users. Besides writing the docs herself, Eva is passionate about creating a culture of documentation within and across technology organizations and loves mentoring others on their writing. Outside of her daily work, Eva is an accomplished conference speaker. She also enjoys learning languages and has been studying Russian for the past five years.

Create Your Supporting Artifacts, page 138

Dawn Parzych

Dawn Parzych is a developer advocate at LaunchDarkly, where she uses her storytelling prowess to write and speak about the intersection of technology and psychology. She enjoys helping people be more successful at work and in life. She makes technical information accessible, avoiding buzzwords and jargon whenever possible. Dawn regularly speaks at conferences and virtual events. Her articles have appeared in numerous technical publications.

The Performance Emergency Fund, page 176

Suhail Patel

Suhail Patel is an engineer on the Platform team at Monzo. He works on surfacing and fixing deviant behavior in core infrastructure components such as Kubernetes, Cassandra, etcd, and much more, across distributed systems. Typically, you'll find Suhail with headphones, listening to electronic music while he works; some have noted a correlation between the beats-per-minute (BPM) of the music and Suhail's thought process.

Effortless Incident Management, page 82
On-Call Rotations that People Want to Join, page 144
The Power of Uniformity, page 164

Jennifer Petoff

Jennifer Petoff is the global head of SRE Education at Google and is based in Dublin, Ireland. She is one of the co-editors of the best-selling book, *Site Reliability Engineering* (*https://oreil.ly/0nWyn*), and lead author of *Training Site Reliability Engineers* (*https://oreil.ly/mYTY1*) (O'Reilly).

Why Training Matters to an SRE Practice and SRE Matters to Your Training Program, page 162

Jake Pittis

Jake Pittis is a software engineer based in Montreal, Canada. When he's not playing jazz piano or macerating peaches, he works on front-end and inter-service networking at Stripe, with a focus on reliability and developer productivity.

Sometimes the Fix Is the Problem, page 99

Bart Ponurkiewicz

Bart Ponurkiewicz is a Senior Site Reliability Engineer at Google working on reliability of mobile applications. In the past few years Bart worked on improving product reliability on multiple teams spanning pipelines, storage systems, and user-facing products like Google Photos. He works best in moments of uncertainty, where abstract situations require quick thinking and creative solutions. Trouble is Bart's middle name as he loves adventures and active lifestyle including paragliding, scuba diving, and riding his motorcycle.

Holistic Approach to Product Reliability, page 107

Ashley Poole

Ashley Poole is an experienced engineer and technical lead with a background across infrastructure, site reliability, and software engineering disciplines. He is an avid site reliability engineering advocate and has a keen focus on improving the developer experience wherever possible. He is passionate about sharing knowledge and has spoken at various user groups and conferences. He is also co-organizer of a software development user group based in the UK.

Solo SRE: Effecting Large-Scale Change as a Single Individual, page 53

Björn "Beorn" Rabenstein

Björn "Beorn" Rabenstein is an engineer at Grafana. He is best known for his ambition to get involved in as many SRE books as possible. Or perhaps for his contributions to the Prometheus project. In previous lives, he was a production engineer at SoundCloud, an actual SRE at Google, and a number cruncher for science.

The Third Age of SRE, page 201

J. Paul Reed

J. Paul Reed began his career in the trenches as a build/release and operations engineer. After launching a successful consulting firm, he now spends his days as a senior applied resilience engineer on Netflix's Critical Operations and Reliability Engineering (CORE) team, focusing on incident analysis, systemic risk identification and mitigation, applied resilience engineering, and human factors expressed in the streaming leader's various sociotechnical systems.

A Word from Software Safety Nerds, page 197

Frances Rees

Frances Rees (née Johnson) serves reliable databases to the Cloud as a senior site reliability engineer at Google Dublin. Previously, she has been the technical lead for SRE on the Google Maps Platform and has cochaired SREcon APAC since 2019. She holds degrees in mechatronic engineering and computer science from the University of Adelaide. Outside of work, she enjoys weaving chainmail (the metal kind), winning Tetris Battle, and attending to two feline overlords.

Dear Future Team, page 36
Why I Hate Our Playbooks, page 86

Tanya Reilly

Tanya Reilly is a principal software engineer in the Architecture group at Squarespace. Before Squarespace, she spent 12 years wrangling infrastructure at Google. In her free time, she likes to code on trains, watch cartoons with her kid, study Arabic, and play guitar (badly). She blogs at *http://noidea.dog*.

Use Your Words, page 32
Test Your Disaster Plan, page 160
That 50% Thing, page 181

David K. Rensin

David K. Rensin is Senior Director of Engineering in the Office of the CFO, where he serves on a small team of technical advisers to Alphabet's CFO. He provides guidance on the appropriate allocation of Google's capital to its various businesses and long-term technical investments. Prior to that, Dave founded Customer Reliability Engineering (CRE) and ran Google's global network capacity planning. He has more than 25 years' experience designing and delivering planet-scale cloud and mobile products. Prior to joining Google, Dave worked at Amazon on its classified (now declassified) C2S project. As an entrepreneur, he has cofounded and sold several businesses, including one (Riverbed Technologies) for more than $1 billion, and has served as an officer in two publicly traded companies (Omnisky and Aether). He is also a best-selling author and editor with 16 US patents to his name. Dave earned a degree in statistics from the University of Maryland and is married with three children.

The Order of Operations for Getting SLO Buy-In, page 140

Jacob Scott

Jacob Scott is a software engineer currently focusing on reliability at Stripe. He is an enthusiastic participant in the resilience engineering community and passionate about how to apply learnings from modern safety science to real, complex sociotechnical systems.

Four Engineers of an SRE Seder, page 8

Ben Sigelman

Ben Sigelman is a co-founder and the CEO at LightStep, a co-creator of Dapper (Google's distributed tracing system), and a co-creator of the OpenTracing and OpenTelemetry projects (both part of the CNCF). Ben's work and interests gravitate toward observability, especially where microservices, high transaction volumes, and large engineering organizations are involved.

Design Goals for SLO Measurement, page 55

Murali Suriar

Murali Suriar is a lapsed computer science graduate, turned network engineer, turned SRE, currently working on storage systems at Google.

An Overlooked Engineering Skill, page 76

Avleen Vig

Avleen Vig is an industry veteran with over 20 years of experience, including 10 years as a remote engineer. As a production engineer at Facebook, he works to build the next-generation infrastructure platforms for the company.

Remotely Productive or Productively Remote, page 119
You See Teams, I See Product, page 174

Salim Virji

Salim Virji is a site reliability engineer at Google. He develops reliable engineering practices and processes for Google's SRE group and has previously developed distributed consensus and storage systems. Salim's interests include distributed systems and machine learning. Salim received an AB in Classics from the University of Chicago.

The Importance of a Management Interface, page 24
When It Comes to Storage, Think Distributed, page 26

Vinessa Wan

Vinessa Wan has been working in product project management for the past 10 years. In her past six years at the *New York Times*, she has worked in R&D and product discovery and now oversees the Operations Engineering portfolio. In her spare time, she loves to hike and play music.

Building Tools for Internal Customers that They Actually Want to Use, page 113
It's About the Individuals and Interactions, page 115
Sneaking in Your DevOps Deliciously, page 127

Hillel Wayne

Hillel Wayne is a formal verification consultant, the author of *Practical TLA+* (*https://oreil.ly/7EdsO*), and a member of the Alloy board. You can find his work at *www.hillelwayne.com*. In his free time, he juggles and makes chocolate. He's legally allowed to deliver babies in Illinois.

The Importance of Formal Specification, page 187

Thai Wood

Thai Wood helps teams build better systems and improve their ability to effectively respond to incidents. A former EMT, he applies his experience managing emergency situations to the software industry. He writes about resilience engineering each week at *ResilienceRoundup.com*.

With Incident Response, Start Small, page 51

Vanessa Yiu

 Vanessa Yiu is a site reliability manager based in London. She has more than a decade of experience in operating enterprise-scale platforms as well as managing global engineering teams. She is a speaker, cochair, and committee member of USENIX SREcon and is involved in a number of organizations that advocate for women in STEM. Outside of the office, Vanessa can most often be found at her workbench, crafting jewelry, or painting and engraving in different forms of art work.

Denise Yu

 Denise Yu is a senior software engineer, currently at GitHub, previously at Pivotal R&D and Mergermarket. She loves growing engineering teams into product-oriented, high-trust, cross-functional organisms. She speaks regularly at conferences and meetups in North America, Europe, and Asia on a wide variety of topics, ranging from continuous delivery to site reliability engineering principles, explained through cats. Outside of software engineering, she enjoys creating digital art, playing Japanese RPGs, and listening to Taylor Swift on endless loop.

Index

A

a student should be able to (ASSBAT), 162-163

abstractions, 77

accidental complexity, 133

ACKs, 22-23

allostatic load, 121

Apache Traffic Server (ATS), 20-21

API, 25, 89, 166

application layer, 20

application programming interface (see API)

architectural analysis, 193-194

ASSBAT (a student should be able to), 162-163

ATS (Apache Traffic Server), 20-21

audits, 49

automation software, 24, 88-89, 93-94

autoscaling, 14

availability, 9, 183-184

B

bandwidth, human, 6

black swan event, 58, 194

Blank-Edelman, David N., 201

blogs, 168-169

brag document, 71-72

Brooks, Fred, 41, 133

bugs, 23, 95, 99, 187
  (see also debugging)

bulkheads, 14

Burgess, Mark, 197

burnout, 38, 40, 50, 90-94, 121, 148, 153, 200

C

caching, 14-15

caching layer, 20-21

capacity, 49

cardinality, 28-29

cascading failures, 150-151

CDN (content delivery network), 20

Challenger Space Shuttle, 46

changes, 59-60, 129-130, 156, 159, 166-167
  (see also cultural changes)

chatbot, 94
  (see also ChatOps)

ChatOps, 93-94

Chesterton's gale, 32-33

CI/CD (continuous integration/continuous delivery), 109

circuit breakers, 14

client satisfaction, 45

cloud-native technologies, 202

code, 181-182

code compliance, 185-186

failovers, 14

failure mode and effects analysis (FMEA), 193

failure mode, effects, and criticality analysis (FMECA), 193

failure model analysis (FMA), 193

failure modes, effects, and diagnostic analysis (FMEDA), 193

fallback plans, 160-161

fallbacks, 14

fdSRE, 157-159

feature flagging, 97

feedback, 7, 66, 113-114, 153
  peer, 72

feedback loops, 38-39, 105, 114, 147, 172

Fermi problems, 125

financial compensation, 41

FMA (failure model analysis), 193

FMEA (failure mode and effects analysis), 193

FMECA (failure mode, effects, and criticality analysis), 193

FMEDA (failure modes, effects, and diagnostic analysis), 193

formal specification, 187-188

formal verification(FV), 186

forward-deployed SRE (see fdSRE)

Fournier, Camille, 6

Frama-C, 186

Fraser, A. G., 192

freshness, 55

Freudenberger, Dr. Herbert, 38

FV (formal verification), 186

G

gaps, 79, 199

generative culture, 7

GFS (Google File System), 24

Google, 201

Google File System (GFS), 24

group chat tools, 93

(see also ChatOps)

H

happiness at work, 41

health, 152
  (see also health checks, mental health, service health)

health checks, 39

hero culture, 142-143, 182

holistic approach, 107-108

HTTP requests, 22

human baseline, 118

I

IC (individual contributor), 119

idempotency, 88

IEC 61508, 183-184

IMOC (Incident Manager On-Call), 80

In Search of Certainty, 197

incentives, 6-7

incident communication channel, 82

incident lead, 82

incident management, 53-54, 80-83, 93
  (see also ChatOps)

incident response, 38, 42, 51-52, 80-81, 99, 118, 148, 197-198
  (see also incident reviews)

incident response plan, 51-52, 85
  (see also runbooks)

incident retrospectives, 147

incident reviews, 99-100

incident-state documents, 33

incidents, 199-200

individual contributor (IC), 119

infrastructure, 13, 49, 86
  (see also infrastructure engineers)

infrastructure engineers, 13

initial public offering (IPO), 30

integrity analysis, 186

Internet of Things (IoT), 108

internet protocol (IP), 131

overprovisioning, 14

P

PagerDuty, 94
pagers, 42-43, 51, 146-149
pair programming, 118
pairing, 6
paradox of preparation, 189
Parser Cache, 20
path complexity, 185
Pennarun, Avery, 124
performance, 7, 123
performance budgets, 176-177
performance reviews, 72
planning (see roadmaps)
playbooks, 33, 86-87
Polyspace, 186
positive incentives, 6-7
PR (pull request), 132
PR descriptions, 32
PRD (product requirements document), 140
prioritization, 14
probability analysis, 2
problem solving, 121-122
product developers, 5
product requirements document (PRD), 140
production, 97-98
production flow rate, 95
productivity, 119
psychological safety, 39
pull request (PR), 132
pull-request reviewer, 32

Q

QOS (quality of service), 123
QPM (queries per minute), 108
quality of service (QOS), 123
queries per minute (QPM), 108
queuing, 14-15

R

RAID (redundant array of independent disks), 26
Rails, 98
read-eval-print-loop (REPL), 74-75
reconstruction, 62
redundant array of independent disks (RAID), 26
release procedures, 54
reliability
    documentation and, 32-33, 84
    impact of, 63, 181
    importance of, 8-9, 45, 57
    need for, 4-5, 49-50, 95-96, 109-110
    supports for, 99-100, 105
reliability stack, 10-11
remote procedure call (RPC), 108
remote teaming, 119-120
remote teams, 175
repeatability, 54
REPL (read-eval-print-loop), 74-75
Request for Comment (RFC), 32
request rate variable, 14
resilience, 14-15
resource gaps, 199
Response tool, 83
responsibility, 8, 78-79
retries, 14
RFC (Request for Comment), 32
risk, 193-196
risk analysis methodology, 193
    (see also architectural analysis, data-driven analysis)
risk diversity, 27
roadmaps, 178-179
RPC (remote procedure call), 108
runbooks, 84-85, 109

S

SA (static analysis), 185-186
safety critical system (SCS), 183-184

About the Editors

Emil Stolarsky and
Jaime Woo

Emil Stolarsky is a site reliability engineer, who previously worked on caching, performance, and disaster recovery at Shopify and the internal Kubernetes platform at DigitalOcean. These days, he's the co-founder of Incident Labs, and in his off-time can be found listening to Flume and fighting his fear of heights by rock climbing.

Jaime Woo began his career as a molecular biologist before working at DigitalOcean, Riot Games, and Shopify—where he launched the engineering communications function. He co-founded Incident Labs, focusing on providing teams with improved SRE tooling to return more time for planned work. He is also an avid lover of dumplings.